TMI

MY LIFE IN SCANDAL

PEREZ HILTON

WITH LEIF ERIKSSON AND MARTIN SVENSSON

CHICAGO
REVIEW
PRESS

Published by Chicago Review Press Incorporated

814 North Franklin Street

Chicago, Illinois 60610

ISBN 978-1-64160-404-8

Library of Congress Cataloging-in-Publication Data

Names: Hilton, Perez, 1978– author. | Eriksson, Leif, 1957– author. |
Svensson, Martin, 1978– author.

Title: TMI : my life in scandal / Perez Hilton with Leif Eriksson, Martin
Svensson.

Other titles: Too much information

Description: Chicago : Chicago Review Press, 2020. | Summary: "The story of
how Mario Lavandeira became Perez Hilton, the world's first celebrity
blogger and the most hated man in Hollywood"— Provided by publisher.

Identifiers: LCCN 2020024462 (print) | LCCN 2020024463 (ebook) | ISBN
9781641604048 (cloth) | ISBN 9781641604055 (adobe pdf) | ISBN
9781641604062 (epub) | ISBN 9781641604079 (kindle edition)

Subjects: LCSH: Hilton, Perez, 1978– | Television personalities—United
States—Biography. | YouTube (Electronic resource)—United
States—Biography. | Bloggers—United States—Biography. |
Celebrities—United States—Biography.

Classification: LCC PN1992.4.H557 A3 2020 (print) | LCC PN1992.4.H557
(ebook) | DDC 818/.603 [B]—dc23

LC record available at https://lccn.loc.gov/2020024462

LC ebook record available at https://lccn.loc.gov/2020024463

Unless otherwise indicated, all images are from the author's collection

Interior design: Jonathan Hahn

Printed in the United States of America

5 4 3 2 1

*"No matter how much of an insider I ever become or am,
I'll still always be an outsider."*
—PEREZ HILTON

"All literature is gossip."

—TRUMAN CAPOTE

CONTENTS

PROLOGUE

It's 2010, and I'm with Lady Gaga at the dress rehearsal for the Much Music Video Awards in Toronto when I hear a woman's voice behind me: "Why have you been writing all those nasty things about me on your website?"

I turn around and see Fergie from the Black Eyed Peas. She's standing just a few feet away from me, at the edge of the stage. From the speakers, I hear the intro to "Paparazzi," and Lady Gaga's voice soon fills the empty venue.

Fergie gestures wildly. "Why are you being so mean?"

I don't really have a good answer for her—which is why I continue to ignore her questions.

Fergie shakes her head and walks away.

The next evening, at the entrance to Universal's after-party, I bump into will.i.am.

"Hey, Perez," he says. "I need you to do me a favor. I need you to never write about my band on your site again."

I take a deep breath before telling him, "Uhh . . . I'll try."

Other people have started to gather around us. I'm tired and sweaty, and the makeup I wore to the awards show is making my face itch.

Will.i.am continues: "Why'd you disrespect me, man?"

I meet his eye for the first time. "I don't have to respect you. You're such a fag. Stop being such a faggot."

Sadly, I don't even have time to regret my words before, from the corner of one eye, I see a man step forward with his fist raised. Everything goes black.

1

The Fat Kid

I escape to Mom's Spanish gossip magazines and
The Oprah Winfrey Show.

I grew up with my mom, dad, maternal grandparents, and little sister in a super suburban neighborhood of Miami called Westchester. Everyone who lived there was the same; the families on both sides of the block were Cuban, and mine was just like all the others. The single-story house we lived in looked the same as all the others, too—aside from the fact that we didn't have a pool, and my bedroom didn't have any windows.

Back then, my name was Mario Lavandeira, born Mario Armando Lavandeira Jr., though I was also known as "the Fat Kid." That's what everyone called me after a couple kids from school started to sneak up behind me and give me embarrassing back fat pinches, laughing at me. Either that or they'd make fun of me in other ways.

But before I get into all that, I need to tell you about the first few years of my life, because they were actually pretty good—and above all, totally carefree. A few blocks from where I lived, there was a place called La Perla Supermarket. I loved going there with my mom, Teresita, and always used to grab a bite to eat in the bakery while she shopped.

Before I was born, she actually worked as a cashier there, and that's how she met my dad, Mario (though everyone called him Mandy, short for his middle name, Armando). They had both moved from Cuba in the late 1960s, back when it was still legal to do so.

My mom's dad used to own a couple of butcher shops in Havana, but when the Castro regime took over, the government confiscated all private businesses and brought them under state control, so he decided to try to create a better life for himself and his family in America. Virtually all of my mom and dad's relatives did the same—it's truly tremendous what the Cuban community managed to accomplish in Miami.

In the mid-1970s, while Mom worked at La Perla, Dad and his parents were living in a rented apartment right down the street, and she would see him almost every day when he went in to buy coffee. Mom was only sixteen at the time, Dad twenty-eight, but he was still living at home—which wasn't unusual for a single Latino man back then. It was four years before they got married, but just two years after that, on March 23, 1978, I was born.

At the time, we were living in a two-room apartment on Southwest Twelfth Avenue in Little Havana. It was a predominantly low-income neighborhood, but there was a great sense of community there, mostly because there was one major thing binding us all together: our culture. Everybody knew everybody,

Roiz Photo Studios

and my mom's parents, Felipe and Elia, lived only a short walk from our apartment.

I loved my grandparents dearly. Most of all, I loved my *abuelo* (grandfather), who was a very affectionate man and almost acted like a second father when Dad was busy working. Whenever they came over to our place, I put on shows just for him, dancing and goofing around, and he always used to encourage me.

———

Mom stopped working pretty soon after I was born, because Dad wanted her to stay home with me. She was happy to do it, but she was never really a domestic person. In fact, my father was the one who cooked for us when he got home from work; he made the best Cuban food in the world. For the holidays we would always have Cuban-style pork, and during the week it was usually rice and beans, breaded beef, or some other variety of meat.

While Dad took care of the cooking, Mom used to talk on the phone with her friends. She loved to gossip and would talk about anything and anyone—about our family, our relatives, friends and acquaintances, neighbors (not much has changed there). The interesting thing is that in the Latino community, the word *gossip* (*chisme* in Spanish) isn't something negative; it's something everyone likes, and even as a kid I could spend hours flicking through Mom's Spanish-language gossip magazines. The truth is that I didn't actually learn to speak English before I went to school.

In any case, Gloria Estefan was the celebrity I obsessed over most around this time, and for my sixth birthday Mom and Dad took me to one of her shows. They were fans of Gloria, too— she's another Cuban from Miami, and Cuban Americans like to think of her as royalty. The show at the Miami-Dade County Auditorium was in two acts, with one intermission, and for the encore they played "Conga," Gloria's biggest hit. I remember they had these huge blow-up balls that they were tossing around the audience as Gloria shouted, "If anyone wants to come do the conga with me, come on up!"

Without pausing to think for a second, I charged up onto the stage. That was the moment when I first realized I was different.

That was the moment when I first realized I was different.

Mom was pregnant with my sister Barbara around this time, and a few months after she was born we moved into a single-story home at 8400 Southwest Twenty-First Street in Westchester, together with Mom's parents. I don't remember much of the move itself, but I do remember immediately loving our new home, which was much bigger than our tiny old apartment. I remember one of our first days there particularly clearly, because I went over to the neighbor boy's place to play.

We were alone in his house and decided to take off our clothes. More accurately, we *thought* we were alone, but his big brother suddenly came charging into the room and my parents found out all about it that very same night.

Not long later, they sent me to a therapist with the aim of trying to make sure I wasn't gay. I guess that shows just how worried they were. I mean, no one from our neighborhood went to therapy.

As far as I was concerned, the therapy sessions were pretty funny. I mean, all that happened was they dropped me off with a woman who, in my eyes, seemed really strange. She just asked all kinds of questions and had me play.

Sadly, the treatment sessions didn't go on for long. After just the second or third session, the therapist asked me to wait outside while she talked to my mom. I could hear her through the door as she said, "You know, your son is exceptionally bright. There's nothing wrong with him."

The kids at school clearly had other ideas, because when I started first grade that fall the other students seemed to decide I was someone they could pick on and bully. Other than giving me back-fat pinches, mocking me, and stealing my school bag and throwing it around between themselves, they started calling me Elvis, because my hair was all big and poofy. Elvis or Barf, after the fat dog-like character in the film *Spaceballs*.

There was only one occasion where I actually stood up for myself and fought back. It happened when a kid refused to stop pushing me in the hall at school—even though I asked him several times. It didn't help, and just a few days later someone yelled, "Hey, Fat Kid!" at me. That name stuck for the rest of my time at school.

Despite all this, my parents were constantly reminding me about the sacrifices they had made to send me to private school. Telling me it was the reason we couldn't afford a fancy car and so on. All in all, it made me quiet and introverted, and when school finished for the day I went straight home to my room and sat on my bed, eating junk food and watching sitcoms and *The Oprah Winfrey Show* until late in the evening. The truth is, I still think of that bedroom as some kind of backdrop for my childhood. The beige wallpaper, the wooden furniture, the blue tiles in my bathroom. And, of course, the TV. Together with Mom's Spanish-language gossip magazines, it became my only window out onto the world.

2

Latino Culture

My parents continue to worry about my feminine side and enroll
me in judo class in an attempt to butch me up.

The older I got, the worse the bullying became, but if I'm
really honest, I don't think they did it because of the way I
looked. I think they did it because I was gay. It wasn't something
anyone ever mentioned, but it was definitely always the elephant
in the room.

The problem was that I couldn't come out. Particularly not
once I started sixth grade and began attending a strict Jesuit all-
boys school where you had to wear a uniform and go to mass,
and where 95 percent of the students were Latino.

During the 1990s, no one ever really talked to us about
homosexuality at school. Not until one day in theology class,
when my teacher said, "You know, there are studies that claim
one in every ten people is gay."

I remember staring at her and thinking, *Wow, is she really*
saying this?

Unfortunately, she crushed what little hope I had in the very next breath, by saying, "But you boys aren't like other boys." The saddest thing about it was that she was a lesbian herself (still in the closet, of course).

Back then, Latino culture as a whole was incredibly *machista*, and that meant it was OK to say bad things about gay people, even if they were members of your own family. I had a gay cousin, and I remember my relatives saying things like "Hope she doesn't bring her girlfriend" whenever we got together for the holidays. I also remember overhearing them talk about another gay relative, saying that they didn't want him in the swimming pool because he had AIDS, and they were worried the kids might catch it.

There was so much ignorance back then, a real lack of education, and it was pretty commonplace to hear jokes about gay people whenever the family got together. I remember one occasion in particular, at home in our living room. I made such an effort to laugh at one of their jokes that I could feel my mouth straining, but I was also terrified they would notice how hurt I actually felt. The reason I remember that occasion so clearly is because just a week or so later, I asked my parents if I could start taking piano lessons. I loved music more than anything, and I desperately wanted to learn an instrument.

It was the fall of sixth grade, and I guess it must have been the weekend, because although it was after ten in the morning, both Mom and Dad were sitting at the kitchen table when I came into the room.

"Can I start piano lessons?" I asked, immediately realizing that I should have kept quiet.

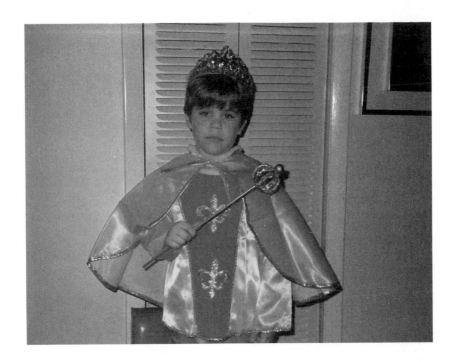

Mom just stared at me before calmly explaining that piano lessons were something little girls did. The very next week, she and Dad enrolled me in judo class instead.

Naturally, I hated it from the moment I first set foot in the club where the lessons took place. The whole place stunk of sweat, and I instinctively began backing out of the room, but Dad—who had given me a ride there—put an arm around my shoulders, trapping me beside him.

Before long, the coach—a short, Asian man whose body was practically square—spotted me. He showed me the way to the changing room, where I reluctantly put on the judo kit Mom had bought for me. I actually felt pretty good in it when I saw myself in the mirror on the wall outside the showers, but that feeling quickly disappeared as I stepped back into the training space.

In that room, as I tried to defend myself, I felt fat and awkward; I couldn't even manage to fall the right way. My parents couldn't help but notice, and eventually they realized they were wasting their money by sending me there.

————————

During this period, I felt much closer to Dad than to Mom. He was a quiet, happy man with a lot of friends. I'd say he was intelligent, too—just not in a formally educated way; he was more self-taught. He read the paper every morning, and since I loved our time together, I read it with him. Strictly speaking, I read the English section and Dad read the Spanish.

It was Dad who taught me how to swim, even if he did do it his own way—by throwing me straight in at the deep end. The first time it happened was during one of our holidays at the Fontainebleau hotel in Miami Beach. I'd always loved the water, and as far as I recall, I was playing in the shallow end of the pool when Dad lifted me up out of the water. I thought he was joking at first, right up until he walked me over to the edge of the deep end and shouted, "Three, two, one, zero!"

Dad didn't give up, and after throwing me into the water for maybe the tenth time at various pools around Miami, I managed to swim back to the edge all on my own.

Next thing I knew, I was flying through the air. I landed on my stomach somewhere in the middle of the pool. I panicked, of course, when I realized I was slowly sinking. I actually remember my vision going dark before someone pulled me back out.

Still, Dad didn't give up, and after throwing me into the water for maybe the tenth time at various pools around Miami, I managed to swim back to the edge all on my own.

———————

Dad made a living by running his own wallpapering business. It was a very blue-collar thing, and I loved joining him on jobs—or just going out in his car as he drove around aimlessly, which was his favorite way to relax. When he later began buying and selling livestock, we drove out to the area around Lake Okeechobee together, to attend livestock auctions.

It's funny, but if an older man walks past me on the street now and I catch a hint of Brut, I always think of those journeys—that was the aftershave Dad patted onto his cheeks with a loud "brrrr" every morning, and that was the scent that always filled our car.

3

The Diamond Earrings

I do what I can to win Mom's attention and love.

If Dad was warm and generous by nature, then Mom was cold and selfish. Maybe it was because her own father had spoiled her. She really was his little princess, and that meant it was now Dad's turn to spoil her. Mom loved and worshipped him, and she really was spoiled. She was also very young, which is probably why she often put herself and her own needs first.

I'll never forget the time I asked whether I could have some of the food from her plate on one of the rare occasions we ate dinner together. I had already scraped mine clean, but I was still hungry. Mom just gave me a weary glance and said, "Ask your dad." She knew he wouldn't hesitate to share with me; that's just the kind of man he was.

Another example of Mom's diva behavior comes from her reaction to the birthday gift I bought her when I was thirteen. I'd managed to save up some money after winning at *lotería*, which was kind of like Cuban bingo. Mom and I both loved playing *lotería* at various relatives' houses—mostly old ladies who liked to talk loudly and in detail about things that probably weren't suitable for a boy's ears.

We used to play *lotería* on Thanksgiving, too, which was something my parents often hosted when I was growing up. We had all the traditional American stuff, Cuban roast pork too, and after we ate we would sit down in the Florida room (a kind of sunroom) to play. It always got really competitive, and we always played for money.

On this particular Thanksgiving, I won sixty dollars, which was a lot of money for a thirteen-year-old kid in Westchester. I also had some money left over from my birthday, and that meant I had enough to be able to buy my mom a super special gift I had seen a few weeks earlier.

That Friday, I went down to the mall behind our house, heading straight for the little jewelry store. I looked the assistant in the eye, pointed to a pair of diamond earrings in the glass case, and said, "I'd like to buy those, please."

The assistant took out the earrings and put them into a nice little box. She then smiled at me.

"Are they a gift?"

I felt my cheeks flush when I nodded.

She wrapped the box in some pretty silver paper and tied it with a violet ribbon. The parcel she handed me weighed almost nothing, but to me, it seemed incredibly heavy as I carried it away.

Mom wasn't home, and my whole body was trembling with

excitement to hear her come through the front door. I'd waited so long to surprise her that the minutes felt like hours.

Eventually, I heard the sound of a key in the lock, and I really had to stop myself from jumping up and running out into the hallway, holding out the gift for her.

She came into the kitchen with a bag from the grocery store in one hand. "You look very secretive," she said as she put down the bag in front of the refrigerator, which was humming quietly.

I couldn't wait any longer, so I got up, walked over to her and held out the gift. My hand was shaking slightly.

"Happy birthday!"

Mom looked down at the present in surprise before she took it.

"What's this, have you bought me a gift?"

She forgot about the food and went to sit down at the table, where she untied the ribbon, tore back the paper, and opened the box.

"They're diamond earrings," I informed her—unnecessarily, I immediately realized, because with the way the sunlight from the kitchen window was glittering on those little rocks, there was no doubting what a great gift I'd given her.

Mom gazed down at the earrings for quite some time without speaking. I took her silence as a sign that she was completely overwhelmed. But then she looked up at me.

"Oh, thank you, but these aren't real diamonds; they're cubic zirconia. I only wear real diamonds."

It was like she had kicked me in the stomach. I couldn't breathe, and it felt like my legs were going to give way beneath

It was like she had kicked me in the stomach.

me. As my eyes welled up, I wondered why she couldn't just have said, "Oh, thank you, I love them," even if she didn't mean it.

I managed to hide my disappointment, but I went straight to the bathroom and locked the door, then sat down on the toilet lid and cried.

4

My Family Is Torn to Pieces

No one tells me anything, but it doesn't take me long to work it out for myself.

In the space of just one week between my first and second years of high school, my family's lives were turned upside down. My grandfather dying was the first thing that happened. He was eighty-six, and he died in bed, with Mom, my grandmother, and me by his side. That's the way everyone should go, if you ask me. Peacefully, at home.

My godmother took me to Panama City Beach in northwest Florida, in an attempt to take my mind off it. Still, the whole thing felt as surreal as it did painful. I couldn't quite process the fact that he was gone, that I would never get to speak to him again, or see him in his armchair in front of the TV, doling out funny and cutting remarks about whatever was on the screen.

That surreal feeling stuck with me the entire journey north, and it was still there the next day as I lay on the beach looking up at an endless blue sky.

Just under a week later, it was time for the next catastrophe. It was early in the morning on July 4, 1993, and my cousin and I had just sat down to eat breakfast when my godmother charged into the dining room at the hotel.

"Go up to your room and pack your things," she said, her face serious. "We have to go home."

Confused, we did as we were told, and before long we were in the car, heading back to Miami. I wanted to ask why we had to go home, but my godmother seemed so tense that I just didn't have the nerve. Instead, I started to fantasize about all kinds of possible explanations for our sudden return.

I was used to the adults keeping unpleasant secrets from me.

It was clear something bad had happened, something really bad, I just couldn't think what it might be. By that point, I was used to the adults keeping unpleasant secrets from me.

When we eventually reached Miami, I realized we weren't heading home via the usual route. I was just about to ask why when my godmother turned back to me and said, "There's something I need to tell you . . ."

The anxiety I had been feeling all day turned to a huge knot in my stomach, and I wanted to cover my eyes when she continued, "Your dad is in the hospital. We're going over there now."

That was all she said, but I didn't dare ask what had happened. My heart was racing so fast that my vision blurred, and as I climbed out of the car in the hospital parking lot, my legs felt both weak and heavy.

No one said a word as we marched toward the hospital entrance and took the elevator up to the ICU. The doors barely had time to open before I saw Mom. One look at her was enough for me to realize just how serious things were.

"Your dad had an aneurysm," she said, doing all she could to hold back the tears. She explained that Dad had fallen ill suddenly, in their bedroom at home. Mom had immediately called for an ambulance, but even though the paramedics were quick to arrive, he was brain dead by the time they reached the hospital.

I remember the mix of terror and grief I felt as I walked into his room alongside Mom. We went over to the bed where he was lying on his back, eyes closed, in the cold glow of a striplight.

It was my dad lying there, connected to all kinds of wires and tubes—and yet somehow, it wasn't him.

I ran out of the room and back into the elevator, hitting all the buttons to make the doors close. I wanted to cry, but for some reason I couldn't. I wanted to scream, but I knew it wouldn't do any good.

Before long, the elevator doors opened. I had gone all the way down to the parking garage, which was completely deserted. The stale air smelled like exhaust fumes and gasoline.

Without thinking about what I was doing, I walked over to one of the cars, yanked down my pants, took out my penis and peed onto the floor beside it.

A few days later, they turned off Dad's respirator.

5

Three Years of Silence

*Mom stops eating and loses a ton of weight, and
I smuggle gay porn from Madrid to Miami.*

I don't think I really knew how to take in what happened, even less how to process it. Instead, I buried the whole thing deep inside myself, and began calling family and friends to let them know about my dad's passing.

For Mom, it was much harder, because when Dad died, a large part of her died, too. It was like the light in her eyes went out, and her personality seemed to fundamentally change. She went from being a chatty, lively woman to someone who was quiet and withdrawn, and she also stopped eating.

Mom barely replied if you asked her anything, and I have a clear memory of finding her at the kitchen table one day in late summer, staring blankly ahead. It was a Friday, and we had some relatives coming over to eat, so I asked her something like, "What's for dinner?"

Mom looked up when I spoke, but she didn't meet my eye. It seemed more like she was staring at a point just behind me.

The thing you need to know is that Mom really loved my dad. I'm actually convinced that she loved him more than she loved me or my sister, and if God had given her the option of letting me die instead, I'm sure she would have taken it.

On top of becoming utterly passive and stick thin, she was also diagnosed with type 2 diabetes and lost most of her hair. Not that we ever talked about it. Maybe things are different today, but in Latino culture back then, no one ever really talked about their feelings.

Still, it was plain to see that the family was a mess. I didn't realize it at the time, but when I look back now it's clear that I was a mess too. As an example, after Mom ignored me in the kitchen that day I got into a fight with my sister. I marched over to the refrigerator and grabbed a box of eggs, turned, and left the kitchen, stomping toward my sister's bedroom.

Barbara (who I've always called Barby) and I had never really gotten along. We fought about everything, called each other names—partly because we were so different, but I guess it was also because of the age gap. I had always been jealous of her and the attention she got from other members of the family who thought she was cute. Still, that doesn't explain why I did what I did.

I got to her room, and before I knew what I was doing, I had thrown one of the eggs at the door. I grabbed another and did the same thing again. I was just about to take out a third egg when Barby flung the door open and glared at me.

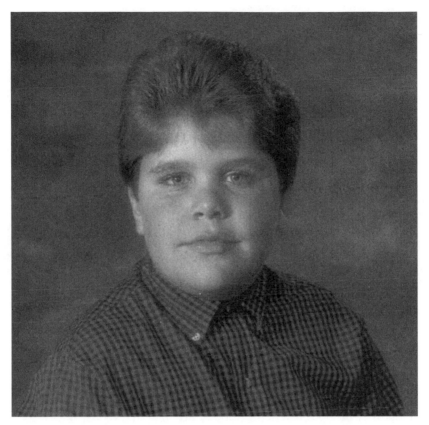

Roiz Photo Studios

She spotted the slimy yellow mess running slowly down her door and fixed her eyes on me. "What the hell are you doing?" she screamed, starting to hit me with clenched fists.

I was stronger than her, of course, and hit her a couple of times in return. We let loose, both of us, and though we had brawled before, this was the worst fight we had ever gotten into.

As I mentioned earlier, school wasn't a place that provided me with any kind of boost, so I continued my passive existence,

That was all I did: watched sitcoms and talk shows, and ate.

practically glued to the television set. That was all I did: watched sitcoms and talk shows, and ate.

Mom used to serve us meals in bed on a tray with built-in legs rather than in the dining room, and I would eat my dinner there after I got home from school. But one day, that all changed: I discovered music.

I'd always had a record player, Mom's old one, so the first music I really got into was hers. Her taste was pretty mainstream: everything from disco to Latin music, Gloria Estefan and Miami Sound Machine to the Beatles. When I was really young, I also bought a vinyl copy of a track called "Sucia." Looking back now, I can't believe I actually bought it, because *sucia* means "dirty woman."

Anyway, it was around this period that music began to play a much bigger and more important role in my life, and I can still remember how I felt when I bought my first two CDs: Madonna's *Erotica* and Ace of Base's *The Sign*. I also started recording music I liked from the radio, and buying magazines like *Entertainment Weekly*, *Vanity Fair*, and *Billboard* from a bookstore in the shopping mall behind our house.

It was around this time that I lost my virginity. It actually happened the summer before, with a classmate. We weren't in love or anything like that, and he is allegedly straight these days. I think it was a case of curiosity for both of us, and once fall term began, we continued to explore one another's bodies.

Sometimes he came over to my place and we had sex in my room. Other times we agreed to meet in the chapel after school. That was the only place no one ever went. There was a wooded area over the road from school, and we sometimes went over there. I'm not just talking kissing and hand jobs: we had oral sex, penetration, everything.

This continued all fall and into winter, before the whole thing fizzled out. Nothing dramatic happened, we just started seeing less and less of one another, and never spoke about what we had done.

When it came to the teachers at the Jesuit school, I got along well with pretty much all of them. I also got an A in virtually every subject without having to try too hard.

There was really only one teacher who didn't like me—my Spanish teacher—but unfortunately she also moderated one of the clubs I was involved with, ALPHA: the arts, literature, photography, humanities, and acting club.

I don't remember all the details, but I do remember that a classmate and I were in her office one day. My classmate wanted to pay for something school-related, and he passed her a blank check. I guess I've never had a filter, because I blurted out, "You shouldn't give anyone a blank check."

I knew right away that our teacher had taken it personally, that she was offended, because she pursed her lips and gave me such a stern look that I felt uneasy, even before she opened her mouth and began yelling at me. I really didn't know what was going on. I mean, I was just repeating what my parents had always taught me. In any case, this was the teacher who accompanied us on a school trip to Madrid the next spring.

Mom was useless with finances and had already spent all the insurance money we got after Dad died, so although I was desperate to go to Spain, we just couldn't afford it. But one day, I remembered hearing someone talk about a book full of addresses for corporations, and it occurred to me that I could write to each of them asking for sponsorship to send me to Spain.

I went to the library that same afternoon and wrote to as many of the corporations as I could. Within a few weeks, I had managed to collect enough money to be able to go after all.

Before we left for Spain, I had no real expectation of being able to explore Madrid on my own, so I was pretty shocked when, after visiting yet another museum, our teacher suddenly said, "You can take the rest of the day off and do whatever you like."

In Europe during the '90s, you could buy porn on virtually every street corner, so the first thing I did was to track down the nearest newsstand to buy stacks of gay porn. Sadly, I didn't realize that VHS tapes in Europe were incompatible with the players in the United States, but at least the porn magazines served their purpose.

I remember being incredibly nervous as we flew back to the States. I was a minor, after all, and terrified about being arrested. My hands were totally damp with sweat and I kept glancing back over my shoulder.

I must have looked unbelievably suspicious, but I was so desperate for masturbation material that I was willing to take the risk. Thankfully I breezed through customs without a hitch, and I hid the porn on top of my closet the minute I got home.

6

NYC:
A Mecca for Gay Men

I come out, learn African dance, and sleep around
without using protection.

In 1996, I moved to New York City to begin studying at NYU. I had a bed in a low-cost dorm, sharing a room with two other students, living as cheaply as I could, but I still didn't have enough money to make ends meet. In fact, the only reason I could even attend college in the first place was because I had a scholarship that paid the tuition. Sadly, I had to cover room and board and everything else myself.

I spent the summer before I left working as a warehouse clerk at a clothing store in Miami, trying to save as much money as I could. My duties involved collecting the hangers left behind after people tried on clothes, then sorting them. The kids' hangers had to go in one basket, the adult ones in another, lingerie hangers in a third, and so on. It was mind-numbingly dull, and it went on for hours on end.

At the end of the day, once the store closed, I also had to clean the bathrooms. I discovered that the women's bathroom was always super dirty, while the men's room was pretty clean. The ladies' room was always full of poop and blood and God knows what else. It was gross, and I often had to stop myself from throwing up.

During my last few months in Miami, I had begun to feel a lot like a prisoner. Like Los Angeles, Miami is a city built for cars, and since I couldn't afford one of my own, I was completely dependent on Mom driving me everywhere. In New York, I could get wherever I wanted on my own, and one of the first places I visited was the Big Cup, a popular gay coffee shop in Chelsea (it sadly no longer exists).

I still didn't have any gay friends at the time, so I guess I went there in the hope of finding a community. At first, however, I didn't dare go in. I had never been to an overtly gay place before, and I remember walking by the entrance several times before summoning up enough courage to go inside. The guys who worked in the Big Cup turned out to be super nice, and after that first day I went there whenever I had a free moment, just to read or do schoolwork.

During my first few months in New York, I also spent a lot of time buying myself new clothes. I became a real pro at thrift shopping. Up until then, Mom had bought all of my clothes—her or other relatives, at Christmas or for my birthday. I'd also had no reason to choose a fashion identity back in Miami. But in New York, that suddenly felt incredibly important, and the first style I adopted during freshman year was "acting student"—fitting, given I was studying acting at NYU.

I also started to lose weight, mostly because I wasn't snacking. Back in Miami, I snacked all the time, plus I ate big meals. In New York, I didn't have the time or the desire. Instead, I started to take dance classes, and I learned the tango, African dance, modern dance; I also made a whole bunch of friends, most of them gay. I went from being practically the only gay I knew to being surprised when someone *wasn't*.

That was why it felt like such a natural moment for me to come out.

As it happened, it was around this time that my little sister started snooping around my room in Miami, and she found all the gay porn I had brought back from Spain, which she took straight to my mom. I have no idea whether Mom had known all along, but she certainly knew now, and when I went home for Christmas she brought it up in the car on the way home from the airport.

She wasn't understanding; she wasn't angry or sad. All she said was, "You're my son and I love you, because I have to love you." It might not have been the warmest of reactions, but it definitely could have been worse. I mean, she didn't say that she rejected me or anything like that. If Dad had still been alive, I can only guess what he would have thought about the whole thing.

At the same time, I knew that Mom must have been worried about what her relatives would say. Maybe she was worried she would never have any grandkids. Plus, during the '90s, AIDS was still a big deal.

In any case, it felt great to be able to be myself in front of my family at last.

The first thing I did when I returned to New York was to get myself a fake ID. It looked anything but genuine, but it worked when my new roommates and I went to the deli behind our dorm to buy booze.

Before long, we also started going out several times during the week, and the bars in New York stayed open until four— at which point we would head to a club, which was open until much later.

This was long before apps like Grindr were invented, so if you wanted to hook up with a guy—which I did, *a lot*—you went to a club. I was often so drunk that I had sex without using a condom, but fortunately I never caught anything a quick pill or shot couldn't cure.

Back then, Chelsea was the gay neighborhood, but the two clubs I associate most with my early years in New York were both in the East Village. One was a place on St. Mark's called Boy Bar; it always had the best drag queen shows. The other was the Pyramid, on Fourth Street. Every Friday, it ran a club night called 1984, which played only '80s music. It was great, so much fun. The doorman would sometimes ask for my ID, but most times not, which I loved.

The doorman would sometimes ask for my ID, but most times not, which I loved.

It was such a different time back then, the era of anything goes. I mean, just take the fact that so many of the gay bars and clubs had dark rooms where you could go to have sex with a stranger. I never really enjoyed that kind of thing, to be honest. I mean . . . I wanted to be able to see whoever I was having sex with.

Aside from my roommates, I mostly partied with my friends from the acting group. We sometimes went to the theater, too. You could get really cheap tickets as a student, and I remember seeing *Rent*—with the original cast—eight times. I also saw my all-time favorite musical, *Hedwig and the Angry Inch*, eight times too.

Back then, my biggest dream was to be in a sitcom. I knew I was hardly likely to be cast as the lead hetero love interest, so instead I fantasized about being the boy next door, the gay best friend.

That's actually still one of my biggest dreams.

7

Downward
Financial Spiral

*I spend six months in Europe, visiting places I've only ever
seen on TV, and get an involuntary golden shower.*

Though my years at NYU were wonderful in many ways, I
was constantly struggling to make ends meet. That's why it
probably wasn't the smartest idea to buy a three-month unlim-
ited train pass while I studied in Madrid during the fall of my
junior year.

It's strange, but when you're young,
you don't think about the future at all.
As you get older, however, it's all you
ever think about. You start obsessing
about the future.

When you're young, you don't think about the future at all.

Anyway, I only had class on Tuesdays and Thursdays, which
meant I could spend the rest of the week visiting places I had only
ever seen on TV.

It was the fall of 1998, and I still didn't have a cell phone. Sitting on the train, I spent my time writing journal entries about my experiences, hopes, and dreams. Sometimes I even wrote poetry or came up with my own lyrics. It was one of the best periods of my life.

The time I spent in Madrid was great, too. I lived in an apartment with a bunch of other kids from NYU, and on top of our history of art classes, we also got to visit various museums, where we saw all kinds of iconic paintings by Picasso and the other artists we were studying.

Still, the train journeys I took on my own were the best. London in particular was a lot of fun, even if I did run into trouble, like when I checked into my hostel and tried to get some sleep. There were four bunk beds in each room, and the Australian guy in the bed above me was so drunk that he was snoring like a horse. It was impossible to get to sleep, and when I eventually managed to doze off, it didn't last long. I woke to the sensation of something dripping from the bed above, right onto my face. I quickly realized it was urine, and that it was now *running* rather than dripping; I began yelling, which also meant I woke the other guys in my room.

"What's going on?" someone grunted.

"The Australian guy is pissing on me!" I shouted back. It was quite a scene.

———

When I got back to New York just before the start of spring term 1999, I took out a second credit card to pay off the debt I had

built up on the one I had been using in Spain. Soon after that, I found myself a three-bedroom apartment at 160 Waverly Place in the West Village.

It was a great location, and it was super cheap. This was before all those rich foreigners started buying up apartments, townhouses, and buildings in New York, making rents skyrocket all over the city. Back then, the area was anything but rich; in fact, it was where the young people and college kids lived. That didn't change the fact that I had to pay rent in advance as well as a huge deposit, and since I couldn't think of any better way to come up with the money, I took a cash advance on my new credit card. That was a huge mistake, of course, because it came with an interest rate of over 20 percent.

In parallel to all this, I was still doing what I could to earn money. I looked after an old man for a while. That was really intense, because I had to help him with everything, from showering and getting dressed to eating.

I also found work as an assistant to Susan Morbido, a DJ who lived on Carmine Street, within walking distance of my apartment. Susan was a loving person, a bit like a sister to me, and I loved spending time with her.

While I worked for Susan, my regular duties involved collecting records she had ordered, picking up her mail, and answering her emails. She also recorded her sets whenever she played, selling them on cassette and CD, so I made those and mailed them out for her.

Susan was an amazing woman with a great sense of humor, and I'll never forget the day she came over to me after being on the road and said that I'd forgotten to take out the trash.

We were in her kitchen at the time, and I stared at her in confusion as I said: "But I just did it."

Susan shook her head. "No, I mean all the porn you downloaded onto my computer."

"Uh . . . OK," I said, feeling my cheeks turn red, my eyes wandering.

Another of the jobs I did back then was behind the bar at the Imperial Theatre. I sucked at it, because I hadn't done any bartender training, and I didn't have a clue how to mix drinks.

They fired me when I decided to go home for Christmas, and I started making money by participating in various focus groups instead. On top of the money, I also got food and other products from these companies. Still, it made no difference how hard I worked: I still couldn't pay off my debts, and I was so poor that spring that I ate nothing but hot dogs for months.

Not long after that, I decided I had no other choice but to take out a new credit card, transferring the balance between them. Before long, I probably had around ten credit cards, all completely maxed out.

8

Moving to L.A.

*I try to make it as an actor but have to settle for being a
slave to a sex-crazed meth head.*

W hen I turned twenty-four in the summer of 2002, I had
no job, no car, and I was $60,000 to $80,000 in debt.
So, I did what any recent graduate would do: I illegally sublet my
NYC apartment and moved to sunny Hollywood, where I just
knew everything would be better. I filed for bankruptcy shortly
thereafter.

Other than the obvious attempt to run away from financial
ruin, the idea behind moving to L.A. was to give myself a better
shot of finding acting roles. Sure, there were opportunities for
that kind of work in New York, but as I mentioned before, my
dream was to get a part in a sitcom, the vast majority of which
were filmed in Los Angeles.

The first problem I ran into was my name, because I didn't
look like a Mario Lavandeira. Or, more accurately, I didn't look
the way people *expected* a Latino man to look, at least for casting

purposes. If they have a specifically Latino character, they're going to cast someone who *looks* Latino. I quickly realized it would be difficult to find any parts—I mean, it wasn't exactly like I had a résumé to give them. The only substantial role I'd done to date was a small part in an episode of *The Sopranos*, right after graduation in 2000.

Sure, it had been super cool to have my own little space in a trailer with my name on the door. And yes, they had great catering. But my part wasn't exactly something to boast about—I literally had two lines. Plus, my hair was bright orange—I dyed it myself, shortly before the shoot; I think it was supposed to be blond.

In any case, we filmed on location at a college in New Jersey. I was playing the part of someone checking tickets at a concert, and I still remember my two lines: "You're robbing a benefit concert, you know that?" and "Most people charged it to their student cards."

Back in New York, I had also been in a couple of student films, and I'd been an extra in a few different soap operas, but that was it, and when I moved to L.A., I got no work at all. My two-bedroom apartment above a garage on Willoughby, between Harper and La Jolla in West Hollywood, didn't cost much, but I needed to make money all the same.

I remember checking the job listings constantly between auditions. I had tried out a few different jobs in New York, so I knew exactly what I *wasn't* suited to—being a waiter or a bartender—but unfortunately for me, that was the most common part-time gig for a kid with dreams of becoming an actor in L.A.

Eventually, I managed to find work as a junior publicist for a small PR agency just a short bike ride away from my apartment. The truth is that during my first eighteen months in L.A., I couldn't afford a car, so I biked everywhere. I practically never left West Hollywood.

The PR agency was based out of the publicist's apartment, and I'll never forget the day I showed up for my first shift. The publicist, who must have been at least ten years older than me, flung open the door and stared at me with a weird, agitated look on his face. He was wearing a badly buttoned white shirt that was too tight around the gut, and his tanned, botoxed forehead was glistening with beads of sweat.

"Come in, come in," he said, waving a hand.

And so I did, stepping into what seemed to be his living room. There was a guy around my age typing away on a laptop, and when he saw me, his face lit up. The publicist hurriedly introduced us.

I had zero experience of working for a PR agency, but clearly that didn't matter, because after asking only a couple of questions the publicist told me the job was mine if I wanted it.

I felt myself cheering inside. Sure, the pay was terrible, but I was just relieved I would be able to afford food and rent while I waited for my big breakthrough into acting. At the same time, I had a weird, nagging anxiety about my new employer, and not long later, I started to realize just how crazy he was.

The first warning sign came when he gave my colleague ecstasy (MDMA or, as the kids call it now, Molly) as a birthday gift. He then paced around the apartment, scratching his head, before suddenly, without a word, charging out through the front door.

The other junior publicist must have noticed how shocked I was, because he quickly turned to me and said, "Just do your work and ignore him."

I quickly realized my boss was a full-blown meth addict.

But that was easier said than done, because I quickly realized my boss was a full-blown meth addict. He also started to invite all kinds of people over for sex while the other junior publicist and I were in the tiny bedroom next door, trying to work. I've never been much of a prude, but I always felt uncomfortable hearing his groans from the bedroom, hearing the thudding against the walls.

––––––

After six months, I managed to find another job, as a publications manager for GLAAD, the Gay & Lesbian Alliance Against Defamation. My work there largely revolved around keeping on top of everything they published: reports, pamphlets, brochures, and so on. But as with the previous job, I wasn't really happy there. I spent all of my time sitting in a tiny cubicle, doing the same thing day in and day out. I also got reprimanded after I started pinning cutouts of hot guys and artists I liked on the walls of my cubicle. They claimed it was a distraction. Not long after that, I quit that job and began looking for a new one.

Despite all my work troubles, there was one good thing that came out of my move to California: a healthier lifestyle. Not only did I lose weight as a result of cycling everywhere, I also signed up as a contestant on a VH1 weight loss special, where I learned to work out like Madonna. I might not have achieved her muscular arms, but I did learn how to meal prep and work out on a dime.

2004

MARK ZUCKERBERG AND HIS COLLEGE ROOMMATES LAUNCH FACEBOOK.

PARIS HILTON'S SEX TAPE LEAKS.

PAGESIXSIXSIX LAUNCHES.

NIPPLEGATE, A.K.A. THE SUPER BOWL XXXVIII HALF-TIME SHOW CONTROVERSY.

ANNA NICOLE SMITH GIVES A SLURRED SPEECH AT THE AMERICAN MUSIC AWARDS.

9

PageSixSixSix

*I go from fiasco to fiasco, with no idea that I'm at
the start of a successful career.*

I had been in L.A. for two years without getting anywhere when, in September 2004, I discovered the world of blogging and decided to give it a try myself. I don't really know why I started writing. Probably just to entertain myself. Whatever the reason, I had zero hopes of anyone actually reading it.

I had just started a new job that ate up practically all my time—as a senior editor at *Instinct*, one of the big gay magazines back then. I was responsible for roughly half the content, while the editor-in-chief looked after the rest. I have to say I really enjoyed the job, partly because I liked editing, and partly because I liked to write and to interview people. The only negative was that I was making just $30,000 a year. Back at GLAAD, I was at $35,000.

That's no excuse for what happened, but it is at least some kind of explanation—alongside the more obvious point: I was young and dumb. **I was young and dumb.**

One of my roles at *Instinct* involved looking after the Books section. I sent out review copies to various reviewers and writers every week, but the volume of books we got sent was so great that we could only manage to review a few of them.

The rest of the books ended up in a huge pile at the office, and one day—in an attempt to boost my meager wage—I decided to try to sell those rejected books. They were just gathering dust in the office, after all.

The only problem was that I had no idea where to sell them. West Hollywood wasn't exactly full of second-hand bookstores— in fact, I couldn't remember having seen a single one. That's when my thoughts turned to Amazon, which was relatively new at the time. Unfortunately, it didn't occur to me to set up an account using a fake name, nor that it might be a problem to sell books that hadn't yet been published.

Before long, someone from our rival—*Out* magazine—saw one of my listings and recognized my name. The guy blabbed to the publishers of several books I had put up for sale, and I was called in to see JR, the head honcho at *Instinct*.

At first, I thought he wanted to talk about an article or even praise me for something I'd done, but instead he shook his head as I walked into his office. "I just had a very unpleasant phone call."

He stared down at the desk in front of him for a moment or two, like he wanted to avoid looking at me. Then he looked up and explained what one of our most important advertisers had just told him. The advertiser happened to be the publisher of several of the books I had illegally put up for sale online. My boss said he didn't understand my behavior at all.

Hoebermann Studio

"How could you do something so stupid?" he asked. He seemed genuinely surprised. The look on his face was the same one a *very* disappointed parent might have while they're telling off their kid.

"Uh . . . I'm so, so sorry," I said. I genuinely meant it, and actually started to cry. I finally understood what a stupid mistake I'd made and what the consequences might be.

Confirming my worries, my boss said, "Well, you're great at your job here, but we've got to let you go. It's out there now. If we'd found out about it first, we could've controlled the story and reprimanded you, but people are now using this against us."

That made me cry even harder. My tears were completely in vain, of course. I had managed to get myself fired from a job that didn't just suit me, but that I also really loved.

Once again, I found myself without an income and with zero savings. Thanksgiving was approaching, and the entire situation seemed completely desperate.

As luck would have it, I was still illegally subletting my apartment in New York City, making a profit, and that meant I could at least pay the rent for my place in California. But that was practically all I could afford, so I needed a job—and fast.

Maybe it was my desperation that helped me actually find a job before all the offices cleared out for the holiday. I have no idea. What I *do* know is that I started working as the main receptionist for the E! Entertainment network almost right away.

I got the job through a temp agency, and it definitely felt like a step down on the career ladder, but I was just thankful I'd managed to find a new source of income. Not only did it help to put food on the table, it also meant I could keep my car, which I'd bought used a few months earlier.

To this day, I have no idea how I actually managed to get my driver's license. I had never driven a car in my life, never taken any lessons, but I managed to pass both the written and the practical test on the first attempt.

I had only been working in reception for a couple weeks when the former supermodel Janice Dickinson came in through the glass doors with her gay assistant in tow. Janice was really popular back then, largely thanks to *America's Next Top Model*—she was one of the judges.

I recognized her right away, but tried hard to hide that as I said, "Welcome, how can I help you?"

Janice flashed me a quick smile. "Do you like my shoes?"

I looked down at them; they were clearly expensive. "I love them," I said.

Janice looked me straight in the eyes and said, "Do you know how many men I had to fuck to get these shoes?"

I shook my head. "I don't, but they're definitely worth it."

She laughed and, in the next breath, asked, "Which way is the bathroom?"

"Down the hall, to the left," I said, pointing toward it.

"Thank you," she said, dumping her enormous purse on the reception desk and heading off toward the ladies' room with the poise and walk of a real professional model. Halfway there, she stopped dead and blurted out, "Shit, I forgot my tampon!"

She turned around and came back over to my desk, rummaged through her purse, found what she was looking for, and set off for the bathroom again. While all this was going on, I was trying to work out what was really happening. I mean, the woman must've stopped ovulating a decade earlier.

Suddenly, all my attention was on what Janice's assistant was doing. Without a shred of embarrassment, and without trying to hide it in the slightest, he had started rifling through her purse. The fact I was only a few feet away from him, watching everything he was doing, didn't seem to bother him in the least.

A satisfied smile appeared on his cherub-like face when he found what he seemed to have been looking for: a prescription bottle full of small pills.

Next thing I knew, he had popped the lid, tipped out a whole bunch of pills, and shoved them into the pocket of his tailor-made jacket. He quickly screwed the lid back onto the bottle and returned it to her purse.

I stared at him, thinking, *Man, this is wild!*

Janice soon returned and picked up her purse from the desk. She smiled at me and headed off to her meeting with the assistant trailing her like a lap dog.

Right there and then, I felt an immediate urge to write about what I had just seen on my blog. That very same evening, I recapped everything on PageSixSixSix.com—the name I had given my new website.

The next day, I was back behind my reception desk when a hot, muscular blond from Human Resources came over and said he wanted to talk to me.

"Sure," I said. Right then, I noticed for the first time that he had one of the security guards with him. The guard followed us over to the elevator, and the three of us went up to the third floor, where the HR guy had his office.

"Wait here," he said to the guard, closing the door so he and I were alone in the room. By then, I had a real sense of unease, but I still didn't know what he wanted to talk to me about.

The HR guy gestured for me to come over to his desk. I did as he wanted, and was still totally confused when he asked me to look at his computer screen.

"Did you write this?"

I was looking at my blog post about Janice and her thieving gay boy assistant, and really didn't understand what was going on. I hadn't for a second thought that anyone—aside from maybe a couple of my friends—would read what I'd written.

Slightly shocked, I cleared my throat and said, "Well . . . uh . . . yeah."

The HR guy got up from his chair, opened the door, and cast me a quick glance.

"You're fired."

2005

YOUTUBE LAUNCHES.

BRAD PITT LEAVES JENNIFER ANISTON FOR ANGELINA JOLIE.

JUDE LAW CHEATS ON SIENNA MILLER WITH THEIR NANNY.

COLIN FARRELL CHECKS INTO REHAB FOR AN ADDICTION TO PAINKILLERS.

10

Star

I earn more than ever before but feel like
a reluctant private detective.

Being fired from two jobs in a row made me so depressed that I no longer wanted to be in L.A. So, in February 2005, I packed up my things and moved back to New York.

I still had my apartment there, so I moved into one of the bedrooms and let my tenants stay in the other two. That meant I was staying there for free, but in order to bring in extra money, I started working as a freelance writer for a couple of the celebrity weeklies, including *In Touch* and *Star* magazines. I also devoted all my spare time to my blog, really trying to make a go of it.

Though I knew people were actually reading it by that point, I didn't care about what was or wasn't appropriate to write. I was a huge fan of pop culture and had always wanted to write about celebrities. The blog was my chance to do

I didn't care about what was or wasn't appropriate to write.

it on my own terms, really setting myself apart from almost all the other bloggers, who mostly wrote some kind of public diary and aired their own incredibly private concerns.

It turned out that my frank, personal style had made an impression, and just before I left L.A., I'd gotten a phone call from a woman who worked on a TV show called *The Insider*. She explained that they were doing a feature on Hollywood's most hated websites.

"What would you say about being mentioned in that context?" she asked me, quickly adding, "Possibly even being crowned the most hated."

I was completely taken aback, but I quickly managed to compose myself. "Well, I don't think I'm the most hated," I said, "But if you wanna put me on TV and make me number one, sure, go for it!"

The feature on *The Insider* brought me new readers, and when I got back to New York, I was offered a permanent position at *Star*. I should have said no, of course. Blogging had made me see that I needed the freedom to do myself justice. At *Star*, you worked within a given template and just had to follow orders.

All the same, the salary they offered me—$55,000 a year— was far too high to turn down. They said I could keep my website, PageSixSixSix, too. Apparently, they didn't view it as a conflict of interest.

Around the same time I began working for *Star*, a huge celebrity story about Renée Zellweger and country singer Kenny Chesney was dominating the headlines. There was speculation

they were going to get married (which they did, later that spring). The story meant I didn't have time to get to know the others in the office before my boss turned to me and said, "Mario, I want you to follow every single step Renée and Kenny take."

"You want me to stalk them?" I asked, half joking and half serious.

The editor nodded gravely.

As a result, my first few weeks at *Star* were spent hanging around hotel lobbies in the hope of catching a glimpse of the couple. The payoff from my efforts was so poor that my boss just shook his head.

But that didn't stop him from sending me on similar, equally degrading missions. I'll never forget that day in early summer when he called me into his office. "Russell Crowe got into a fight at a hotel in SoHo. He's been arrested. I want you to go down there and find out exactly what happened."

"Why me?" I asked.

"Well, you speak Spanish, and the employees at the Mercer are Latino, so go try to get more information!"

With a near chronic sense of unease, I headed down to the hotel and began snooping around, asking both cleaners and receptionists what had happened. They didn't exactly welcome me with open arms, and after just thirty or so minutes, I felt a hand on my shoulder. I whipped around and found myself face to face with hotel security.

"Please don't call the police," I groaned, giving him a pleading look. "I'm just trying to do my job!" I buried my face in my hands. "Oh my God, I feel so ashamed!"

The security guard just shook his head, grabbed my arm, and marched me out of the hotel.

I got to a point where I hated my job and my life so much that I wanted to die. In my despair, I called Mom and told her exactly how I felt. I spilled my heart, tears running down my cheeks, but was met by silence on the other end of the line.

Eventually, she said, "My son, that is why they call it work. They don't call it happy."

There wasn't much I could say to that, and we ended the call. Somewhere deep down, I knew what Mom meant, but there was no chance I was going to spend the next fifty years doing a job that just made me unhappy.

As time passed, I became so depressed that I had trouble even getting up in the morning. When I did eventually drag myself out of bed, I would sit in the fetal position in the shower for a whole hour before I could bring myself to head down to the office, where new meaningless tasks awaited me. Sometimes I would have to call up a bunch of experts to ask them whether they thought Nicole Richie looked underweight, for example, or to find out how dangerous Lindsay Lohan's lifestyle really was.

In the end, I had no choice but to seek help at Saint Vincent's community hospital (which has since closed down). The reason I chose that particular hospital was that I had no health insurance at the time—and it had come back to bite me. I barely even made it into the doctor's office before she took one look at me and said that I was bipolar.

Of course, you can't just diagnose someone as bipolar without really examining them first, but I didn't know that, so I said, "Huh, how do you know?"

"I could see it a mile off," she replied, writing me a prescription for pills.

If I had known better, I never would have taken them, but I was in such a bad place that I did as she said without questioning it. Within just a few days, I was feeling worse than ever, but I kept taking the pills. I felt like a zombie—completely numb to the world—and a few weeks later, I decided I couldn't take it anymore and stopped taking the medication. I realized I would rather be depressed than not feel anything at all. Luckily, I managed to keep my website going. It was the one lifeline I had to cling to, and I remember that I began to ask my colleagues whether they thought I should quit and focus on that instead.

My coworkers just told me: "No, don't quit! Don't quit! Nobody's making money on the Internet!"

One thing I learned, right there and then, was that you should never tell your colleagues that you're planning to quit unless you actually want to get fired. The editor-in-chief found out, of course, and put me out of my misery. I was left without a regular income once more.

11

The Coffee Bean &
Tea Leaf

I scoop the world and change my name to Perez Hilton.

The problems really did come crashing down on me after that. Shortly before I was booted from *Star*, the *New York Post* sued me for using the name PageSixSixSix—they had their own gossip column called PageSix, you see. Since I couldn't afford a lawyer, I had no choice but to give up the domain, and I took the opportunity to change my own name in the process.

One reason for the change was that I wanted to protect myself from all the crazies out there by using a pseudonym. It actually turned out to be a smart move, considering all the death threats I got when I outed Clay Aiken, a contestant on *American Idol*. I also wanted to create a character who was separate from me as a private individual. The "Perez" in me was the outsider, the Latino guy, the homosexual, the person who stuck out, and the "Hilton" referred to Hollywood, the mainstream.

Rebranding my website also helped people understand what I was all about, even if they had no idea who I was or what I did. That became particularly clear in May 2005, when the entire site crashed. It happened around the time Brad Pitt and Angelina Jolie went public with their relationship—a very strategic decision on their part, or more specifically on Angelina's, since she was the one who had decided to control the media attention right then.

Anyway, they had flown to Africa together on vacation, and spent several days at the beach. A paparazzo took a whole bunch of pictures of them, but he didn't immediately put them up for sale like he usually would. In fact, he didn't do it until Brad and Angelina had left the country and flown home. The whole thing, in other words, had been arranged by the couple and the photo agency.

I had a source who worked as a journalist for one of the celebrity gossip magazines in the UK, and he told me about both the trip and the photographs, which were (obviously) in huge demand. That same day, I published a story about Brad and Angelina's vacation on my website. The same source in England leaked the images to me (his own magazine was outbid and couldn't run them), and before long, I had published them on my site, before anyone else.

Back then, online security wasn't anywhere near as sophisticated as it is now. These days, you don't share paparazzi photos in emails—you upload them to a secure website with your watermark splashed right across the image. They're all low-resolution, which means they can't be enlarged. But in 2005, I didn't face any of those barriers, so I was first to break the Brad and

Angelina story. I also gave them the nickname Brangelina. It was a global scoop!

Suddenly, all the magazines wanted to write about me, and my visitor traffic rose dramatically overnight, causing the entire site to crash.

I was first to break the Brad and Angelina story. I also gave them the nickname Brangelina.

With my new public persona in place, things finally started *happening* for me, and in late 2005 I moved back to Los Angeles, with a better apartment on Hayworth Avenue, just north of Sunset, and a better outlook.

I still didn't have much money at that point, so I didn't bother to furnish the place properly—nor would I, going forward. All I had was a bed and a recliner chair—I didn't even have a television—but that didn't bother me at all. Especially since I was working all the time anyway.

One thing I did need was access to the Internet, but when I called the cable company on one of my first days in the new place, I realized I couldn't afford for them to come over and install it for me. I mentioned this to the guy on the other end of the line.

"No problem," he said. "We'll send you the kit, and you can install it yourself."

But that didn't really work for me either. I'm not a computer savvy guy; I don't know much about technology or any of that stuff. So, I started going down to the Coffee Bean & Tea Leaf on Sunset and Fairfax instead. They had free Wi-Fi, and it was just a short walk from my place.

I remember that the coffee shop opened at 6:00 in the morning, but I was usually there at 5:30, because their Wi-Fi also worked if you sat just outside the door. What people might not realize is that in November L.A. is cold and dark at that time of the morning. Homeless people would walk by staring at me, and at first the staff seemed to be wondering what I was doing there when they arrived to open up for the day.

Over time, it kind of became my thing, and everyone knew I was working out of there. All kinds of people started to show up—celebrities who wanted to release something to the public, and journalists wanting to find out more about who I was. In fact, one of the first people to come down there and talk to me early one morning was Lindsay Lohan.

She was filming something in L.A. at the time, but seemingly she kept showing up late to set. The director eventually decided he'd had enough and wrote an open letter telling her to get her act together. When she came down to the Coffee Bean that morning, it was to explain that she was en route to set, and that she was on time.

"I don't have time to stay," she said with a laugh. "I'll never make it if I do."

And just like that, she was gone.

This was the fall when I made it my mission to be everywhere that the celebrities were. I remember thinking, *If I start attending all these events, people will say, "He doesn't just talk about celebrities; he moves in the same circles as them."*

It's worth remembering that there were a lot more parties back then, because people needed to drum up attention for their personal brands. These days, a company simply needs to pay an influencer to talk about their new product, or launch a digital marketing campaign. But social media didn't exist then, and that meant the parties were a pretty big deal.

I attended the parties, not only to make myself visible but also to take pictures. If I'm honest, I felt anything but comfortable at them. I often worried that people would boo me or that the photographers would try to pick a fight as I walked the red carpet, since I used to steal their pictures.

For the most part, however, my working days were spent at the Coffee Bean & Tea Leaf. I quickly settled into a routine: I was there before they opened, and always sat at the table by the bathroom, next to the power outlet, so I could keep my laptop charged; they only had one outlet in the entire store. I got my Ice Blended, uploaded pictures, wrote, and ate lunch next door, at a now-closed Baja Fresh. In the afternoon, I got back to it, either working in the Coffee Bean until it closed for the day or heading off to an event.

Eventually, all of my hard work began to pay off financially—first from Google Ads and then from another company that started selling my ads. Slowly but surely, I managed to make a living from my work.

12

———

A Real Friend?

I make friends with a TV star, and a Scientologist
accuses me of being a pedophile.

Someone I hung out with a lot around this time was Amanda Bynes. She was only nineteen when I first met her, but she was already an established star. She made her TV debut when she was just seven years old, and then got her own show, *The Amanda Show*, at thirteen. In the years that followed, she played leading roles in teen comedies like *Big Fat Liar* and *What a Girl Wants*.

In the fall of 2005, when she sent me a message to say she was a fan of my site, I was beside myself. It was so crazy and cool. I replied immediately, and that was the start of a long period of exchanging messages, ultimately developing into a close friendship.

"Why don't you come see me at work?" she wrote one day. At the time, she was one of the leads in a sitcom called *What I Like About You.*

"Sure!" I told her. It felt genuinely great to go to the studio the next day and meet her (and the other actors) for the first time. Amanda smiled when she saw me, and gave me a big hug like we had known one another for years.

Before long, she and many others began showing up at the Coffee Bean. I always loved it when Amanda turned up—something that can't be said of people like Nicole Richie, who would storm into the coffee shop and scream, "You're so fucking mean!" making everyone else turn and stare.

Nicole Richie . . . would storm into the coffee shop and scream, "You're so fucking mean!"

It wasn't great when a bailiff turned up to serve me a lawsuit, either.

A few days after that I was waiting for Amanda so we could go out to lunch, when the door opened and a man in an ugly, ill-fitting shirt came in and peered around the room. His eyes sought me out, and there was something about the way he was looking at me that immediately put me on edge. In truth, it wasn't just the way he was looking at me that made me tense up and slowly close my laptop—it was everything about him: his posture and the way he resolutely began walking toward me.

"You won't get away with attacking my faith!" he shouted, pausing a few feet from my table.

"Your faith?" I mumbled as I tried to prepare myself for whatever came next.

"Scientology!" he yelled, becoming the latest in a long line of people who have caused a scene around me in the coffee house.

I thought for a moment, and quickly remembered that I'd written a piece about the hold the Church of Scientology seemed to have over certain film stars. I didn't recall exactly what I wrote, but I was pretty sure I hadn't been particularly respectful.

"I'm sorry if I upset you," I said, raising my hands in what I hoped was a disarming gesture, "but there's a thing called free speech in this country."

The man stared at me with a look of disgust on his face, and if he hadn't been so obviously crazy, I probably would have been a little uncomfortable. He shook his fist at me and yelled, a string of saliva swinging from his mouth: "You're a pedophile!"

My jaw dropped, because it was a completely insane accusation. Despite that, I felt a sudden wave of paralyzing panic wash over me. I realized that everyone else in the coffee shop had heard what he had said and that they might also believe him. I saw people staring at me with wide eyes.

Surely they can't . . . I found myself thinking, though I knew all too well how easily suspicions can take hold and grow into truths.

The man raised his fist one last time and repeated his accusation so loudly that it could probably be heard out on the street, before turning on his heel and practically making people leap out of his way as he stormed out.

I sat there in complete shock, watching him leave and trying in vain to process what just happened. I quickly realized that everyone was still staring at me, and an icy chill spread through my body.

I wanted to open my mouth and explain that what he had said wasn't true, that it was so far from the truth that I was just as shocked as they were. But for some reason, I couldn't manage a single word, and before I knew it, everyone had returned to their conversations, the baristas taking orders again, clearing dirty cups away.

Right then, Amanda came in through the door and made her way over to my table. "Hi," she said with a frown. "Are you OK? You look like a complete wreck."

I breathed out for the first time in what felt like a long while and said, "Some guy just called me a pedophile."

"You're kidding," Amanda said, sitting down opposite me.

I shook my head.

"Seriously, this place . . . if you're not already crazy, it makes you go crazy," she sighed. What neither of us knew in that moment was that her words were an ominous prophecy of sorts.

Just a few years later, Amanda spiraled completely out of control. She went from being the perfect friend I could go out to dinner with any time, who I could call to talk about nothing in particular, to entering the same self-destructive, unpredictable patterns of substance abuse as so many other young stars. As a result, we didn't just drift apart, we actually fell out.

That was largely down to my job, of course. Because once Amanda lost control and began causing one scandal after another, it became virtually impossible for me *not* to report on it. Amanda was acting out very publicly—and it wasn't a one-off. Before long, all the bridges between us were fully and irreversibly burned.

2006

MEL B CLAIMS THAT EDDIE MURPHY IS THE FATHER OF HER UNBORN CHILD.

TWITTER LAUNCHES.

MEL GIBSON CLAIMS THAT JEWS ARE RESPONSIBLE FOR EVERY WAR.

REESE WITHERSPOON FILES FOR DIVORCE FROM RYAN PHILLIPPE, CITING IRRECONCILABLE DIFFERENCES, THOUGH RUMORS IMMEDIATELY BEGIN TO CIRCULATE THAT PHILLIPPE'S HARD-PARTYING WAYS AND ALLEGED AFFAIR WITH AUSTRALIAN ACTRESS ABBIE CORNISH LED TO THE FAMOUS COUPLE'S SPLIT.

FORMER NSYNC MEMBER LANCE BASS COMES OUT OF THE CLOSET.

NICOLE RICHIE IS ARRESTED ON SUSPICION OF DRIVING UNDER THE INFLUENCE OF ALCOHOL, AND SHE ALLEGEDLY ADMITS TO OFFICERS THAT SHE IS UNDER THE INFLUENCE OF MARIJUANA AND VICODIN.

13

A Hot Mess

Hollywood's number-one bad girl takes me and
Kim Kardashian under her wing.

In May 2006, I decided on a whim to go to the Cannes Film Festival. I didn't have any contacts there, but I did what I could,
inviting myself to a bunch of parties and eventually winding up
being photographed with Paris Hilton.

I had met Paris for the first time the September before, at
New York Fashion Week, and in November of that year *In Touch*
magazine flew me to Las Vegas to cover the opening of a new
nightclub called Body English, which she was hosting. Paris had
just broken up with one of the two Greek men she had been
engaged to, and when she turned up on the red carpet that night,
she didn't want to be interviewed. Not until she saw me, in any
case. I ended up landing the only interview with her, and we
exchanged numbers. At the time, Paris was huge.

In a sense, I guess you could say that she took me under her
wing, and I always wrote positive things about her. Primarily

because she never bothered to sue me for using "Perez Hilton," even though she definitely could have.

A few months after I got home, Paris got in touch and asked whether I would like to come down to the recording studio and listen to the music she had been working on. She never went through her publicist; Paris was friends with all the celebrity journalists, and she always texted them herself. It's pretty similar to the relationship she has with a bunch of Instagram influencers now—it's all because she wants to grow her Instagram page.

I knew Paris was using me, but I also didn't care; I was using her, too. I mean, I was a blogger who was hanging out with Paris Hilton. Years later, when I started hanging out with Adele, it was far worse, because I thought she genuinely liked me.

I knew Paris was using me, but I also didn't care; I was using her, too.

In any case, Paris and I started going out together pretty often, and in August of that year, she released her self-titled album, which we celebrated in Vegas. It was a fun evening, and the fact that she insisted that the DJs play her record (which she had brought along) wherever we went made it even better—and funnier.

The first club we went to that evening was Pure in Caesars Palace (it's known as OMNIA these days), and I'll never forget the way Paris ran straight over to the DJ booth and shouted, "Play track three!" shoving the CD in the guy's face.

———

We often used to party at Paris's house, too. Between 2000 and 2010, Paris threw a party virtually every weekend, inviting so many people over once the clubs closed that her house on Kings Road, close to Sunset, was always packed until seven, eight, sometimes even nine o'clock in the morning.

People chatted in groups, there was a DJ playing music, and in the middle of the living room, Paris had a stripper pole that someone was always amusing themselves and the others on (including Paris's aunt Kyle Richards, who would go on to star as one of *The Real Housewives of Beverly Hills*). I'm sure you're curious about drug use, but to be honest, I never saw Paris do any hard drugs. She was, however, one of the biggest stoners I ever met

> "When people you don't even know hate you, that's when you know you're the best."
> —Paris Hilton

in my whole life. She used to smoke weed every day, from first thing in the morning till late in the evening—a wake-and-baker, as they call 'em.

I loved it there. I never drank much and didn't touch any of the drugs, though I knew they were being done. I was always in work mode, after all, so I simply couldn't allow myself to get sloppy around those people. Plus, I always had to work the next day. Always—I never took a day off. But I would always give them a big grin when I saw them leaving the bathroom in pairs or groups.

It was different for Paris, who in 2006 was a real hot mess. I mean, she was arrested later that year for driving under the influence, and spent three days in prison in 2007 for violating the terms of her probation. The idea of "Hollywood bad girls" was minted largely because of her. The paparazzi followed her everywhere, and the magazines wrote about her every day. They kept doing it until she wore out both her face and her name, and then they all got bored simultaneously.

Yes, Paris is still iconic, but she's no longer hot, and she's no longer a mess. Back then, she was at least as famous as Kim Kardashian is now. In fact, if you ask me, Paris *made* Kim. Many people think it was the sex tape that gave Kim Kardashian her big break, but that isn't right.

In the fall of 2006, Paris made Kim her BFF in much the same way she had done with me. Don't ask me why, but Paris more or less adopted Kim, traveling the world with her and constantly being snapped next to her. If Paris hadn't done that, no one would have cared about Kim's sex tape, but since she was Paris Hilton's BFF, everyone knew who she was.

Several years later, I was featured as a character in Kim's KKH app (Kim Kardashian's Hollywood game, in other words), which was pretty cool. The only problem was that I got pretty sick of Kylie Jenner at around the same time. It felt like she was everywhere, and I didn't like what I was consuming.

On social media, I wrote, "To my fellow media: Can we take a Kardashian break? At least for a week? No Kardashian coverage this coming Mon–Fri? Will anyone join me???" I called my little campaign a Kardashian Kleanse, and other people seemed to feel the same way as I did, because I got a lot of positive responses—from everyone but Kim, that is.

It was stupid of me, and in hindsight, I really regret it. We had a good working relationship, but as attentive readers might have noticed, my behavior often had a certain self-destructive pattern to it. I was impulsive, and didn't think things through before doing them.

Kim removed me from her game not long after.

I'm still in touch with Paris, and actually talked about her in one of my daily videos recently. In the description, I wrote that I wanted her to make a comeback, and a day or two later she called me up, sounding really serious.

"I want you to change the word comeback."

"Why?" I asked, completely lost.

"Because I never went away."

14

RIP

Amy Winehouse and I visit a record store and eat dinner at McDonald's, and I try to interview her while she's high on drugs.

I met Amy Winehouse for the first time in London at a fashion magazine party in late 2006. At that point in time, I was in London pretty often, because I had become—in the most unlikely of ways—good friends with the owner of a hotel there.

It all started when the hotel owner's girlfriend sent me some fan mail (by email, of course). That in itself wasn't so strange, but her boyfriend also started getting in touch to share his appreciation. At first I thought he was being ironic, but I quickly realized that he genuinely liked the things I wrote, and so we kept in touch. He told me he owned a boutique hotel in West London (the now-closed Hempel Hotel) and that I was welcome to stay there whenever I wanted—for free.

"Really?" I wrote back, suddenly suspicious, not used to that kind of generosity.

"Of course," he replied. "Come whenever you like. Just let me know a few days in advance."

London had been one of my favorite cities ever since I went there during college, so being given the opportunity to stay there for free felt almost too good to be true. But when I flew over there a month or two later, I discovered that my new friend was also covering the costs of room service while I was there. I really can't express how grateful I was for that and for giving me the ability to explore London and attend events there. I made new contacts and found a whole load of exciting content for the site. If you're reading this, Paul Murtagh, you're awesome!

It was at one of these events that I met Amy for the first time. Kelly Osbourne was actually the one who introduced us. Kelly and I had known one another a while, and I had written several positive pieces about Amy since she released her first record in late 2003.

I had been struck by her unique voice, among many other things, and began to follow her career. I remember watching her on a British TV show in which she and the host sang a cover of Michael Jackson's "Beat It" together. Amy was so drunk she was slurring, and she forgot the words midsong. She could barely even stand up straight. The poor host kept glancing over at Amy with a look of panic in her eyes, and though it pained me to watch, the whole thing was just *soooo* rock 'n' roll.

I had a flashback of that moment when Amy and I started

> *"I love to live . . . and I live to love."*
> —Amy Winehouse

chatting at the party. I liked her right away. There was something fragile and rebellious about her, and her style was so deliberate, with the beehive hair and those clothes that had already become her signature.

———

The next time I bumped into her was in Austin, and then we met for a third time just a few weeks later, at my birthday party at the Roxy in L.A. in March 2007. We began to develop a friendship. Like I said, I was genuinely fond of her, and the feeling seemed to be mutual. I have to say I didn't like her boyfriend, but later that spring they got married.

I saw the two of them again at Lollapalooza in Chicago in early August. Amy was headlining the festival, and I planned to interview her for a series of TV specials I was doing for VH1, flying in with a film crew from L.A.

We set up for the interview in my suite at the Hard Rock Hotel, and I sat down and waited for over an hour before I finally heard a knock at the door. I got a real shock when I opened it. Amy had changed so much in just a few months, and she really did look sick. Her dodgy husband was with her, but he didn't say a word.

"Hi," she mumbled shyly, absently, giving me a quick hug before sailing into the room.

Her husband nodded but didn't look at me, and I felt a knot of anxiety in my stomach—a knot that grew as Amy announced that she needed to go to the bathroom before we started the interview.

"Sure," I said, casting a quick glance at my increasingly impatient film crew. "No problem."

Next thing I knew, Amy and her husband had disappeared into the bathroom together, locking the door behind them.

My immediate, panicked thought was *I hope to God they're just having sex in there!* I didn't even need to look at the team to know they were thinking the exact same thing: they're doing drugs.

While we waited, we sat on the two couches in another part of the room. No one said a word, we were all just trying to work out what was going on in there. We couldn't hear anything from the bathroom, and time continued to pass. The room was hot from all the lights, and I was stressed, wringing my sweaty palms as I checked the time.

Eventually, the bathroom door opened and Amy and her husband came out. As she sat down next to me and we started the interview, I didn't need to wonder any longer. Amy was obviously high, and there was nothing I could do about it. Instead, I put all my effort into getting enough material to cut it together into something we could show.

Amy was obviously high, and there was nothing I could do about it.

Later, once Amy and her husband left the suite, everyone relaxed. I sat numbly for a long time, torn between a number of conflicting feelings. On the one hand, I was furious at Amy for letting that idiot drag her into trouble, threatening her career, but I also felt a strong sense of concern for her.

I had only just gotten back to L.A. when I heard from her again.

"Hey, it's me, Amy," she said. Thankfully she sounded much more alert than she had that afternoon in the suite. "Want to hang out?" she continued.

"Sure. When?"

"Tonight?"

I met her at the Coffee Bean in West Hollywood a few hours later—without her husband this time, fortunately. Apparently, he was back home in London. She explained that they had gotten into a fight a few days earlier, which didn't surprise me, because their relationship seemed anything but healthy.

In any case, we had fun that evening, and the next morning, as I sat working in the Coffee Bean, she turned up again. Though it wasn't particularly warm outside, she was wearing nothing but a pair of tiny denim shorts, a tank top, and some ballet pumps.

"Hey," I said in surprise. "You're up already?"

Amy nodded and explained that she was staying at Chateau Marmont on Sunset, which wasn't too far away.

"How did you get here?" I asked.

"I walked."

"You *walked*?" I said skeptically, adding, "*Alone?*" I searched the room in vain for some kind of bodyguard or assistant from her label. Unlike many of the other stars, Amy didn't make a big deal of the fact she was famous. In fact, she always looked exactly like she did onstage or on her records.

"Do you want anything? Coffee?" I asked.

Amy shook her head and said she felt like going to visit some of the record stores nearby.

"Cool," I said, closing my laptop.

We walked over to the Virgin Megastore, and the minute we got inside, Amy marched right up to one of the guys who worked there.

"Where's the blues section?" she asked.

The guy recognized her immediately and couldn't manage to say a word, he just pointed to an area toward the back of the store.

"Thank you," said Amy, marching over there. I followed her, fascinated by how confident she seemed in what she was looking for. Within just a few minutes, she had picked out a whole stack of CDs—maybe ten or twelve in total.

"OK, I'm done," she said, heading for the checkout.

The same guy who had given her directions earlier now ran everything through the register, and as Amy passed him her card, he suddenly seemed incredibly embarrassed. "Uh . . . " he said, "it . . . uh, doesn't seem to work."

At that point, it was Amy's turn to look embarrassed, so I quickly said, "I've got it, I'll pay."

"What do you want to do now?" I asked once we left the store.

"I think I need to eat," she said.

My eyes scanned the other side of the street, and I pointed to the McDonald's on Crescent Heights Boulevard. "Will that do?" I asked.

Amy nodded, and we crossed the street and headed inside.

Yet again, I was fascinated by the way she behaved: she bought a ton of junk food, whereas I ordered only a Diet Coke. I found us a quiet table where we wouldn't be the center of attention (which wasn't possible).

While we, or Amy, ate, she became increasingly preoccupied by a text message conversation. It was clearly getting to her, because she alternated between swearing nonstop and sighing deeply.

Eventually, she must have realized she was being a little rude, because she said, "Sorry, it's just my husband. He's such an idiot."

"Well," I said. "Maybe you should think about—"

"No," she interrupted me. "I love him."

She kept texting and cursing him for the rest of the day, and it made no difference what I tried to tell her, she defended him regardless.

Somewhere, deep down, I thought it was great she was so loyal, but I could also see the danger in it. He clearly wasn't good for her, and I wasn't the least bit surprised when she died—just incredibly sad. The only thing that surprised me was that she didn't die of an overdose. She drank herself to death and died of heart failure.

2007

ANNA NICOLE SMITH DIES.

LINDSAY LOHAN CHECKS INTO THREE DIFFERENT REHAB CENTERS.

BRITNEY SPEARS SHAVES HER HEAD.

BRITNEY LOSES CUSTODY OF HER SONS.

DAVID HASSELHOFF'S DRUNKEN VIDEO LEAKS.

CAMERON DIAZ AND JUSTIN TIMBERLAKE BREAK UP.

OWEN WILSON TRIES TO COMMIT SUICIDE.

15

My Twenty-Ninth Birthday Party

*The crowd in Times Square wears Pampers, and I have a very
unusual night with Christina Aguilera and her friends.*

In many ways, 2007 was a strange, overwhelming year for me,
and it all started with John Mayer putting his tongue in my
mouth. It was December 31, 2006, and I was in New York to
cohost MTV's *New Year's Eve* from Times Square.

As I mentioned earlier, I had grown up watching MTV, so
it was a big deal to have been entrusted with that honor. Still, I
felt more nervous than flattered when I arrived at the enormous
studio in the MTV building next to Times Square. It was a huge
production, with hundreds of people running around doing God
knows what. There were already thousands of people outside,
hoping to watch the show and join in the countdown with us.

"So what happens if anyone out there needs to use a bathroom?" I asked the studio manager as she went through the evening's schedule with me.

"They're all wearing Pampers."

I stared at her in shock. "Pampers? You can't be serious—the crowd wear diapers during the show?"

"Welcome to TV," she said, patting me on the shoulder before turning and walking away.

Everything went according to plan that evening, even if I was having trouble processing the information the studio manager had given me. But as the clock approached midnight, I realized that the diapers really did serve a purpose. There was no escaping the hysterical crowd, so when they needed to pee it was just a case of letting go.

Still, I kept smiling, I did my job, and the minute the show was over, I hurried over to the next party, which I was cohosting with Christina Aguilera. I didn't know her very well at the time, but I quickly realized we had great chemistry, and when we finished at around two o'clock, we decided to head over to a nightclub she knew in Chelsea.

In truth, I was exhausted after such a long day, but my mind was racing. It was only once I had been ushered into the club and through to the VIP area that I slumped onto a couch and felt a welcome sense of calm settle over me.

Before long, I had a drink in my hand, and as I sipped it I saw that Christina was chatting to Jessica Simpson, who was with her then boyfriend, John Mayer. She waved me over.

I had met Jessica before, and I knew she really loved to

drink—a lot. Her sister was the same. Her mom and dad, too—the whole family really loved drinking a lot. We always had a lot of fun with them when we hung out at events.

I'd never met John before, but the minute Jessica introduced us, he began chatting to me. I have no idea what the conversation was about, but I do remember how close he was to me, and how he slumped down between me and Jessica on the couch. It was almost like he had been waiting to meet me.

I was both surprised and flattered, and quickly joined in the conversation, which was jumping around between topics. Suddenly, he leaned in to me and said, "I like to watch gay porn, you know."

> **Suddenly, he leaned in to me and said, "I like to watch gay porn, you know."**

"Oh . . . really?" I said, taking a quick sip of my drink to hide how surprised I was.

"Yeah," he said, leaning even closer. "My favorite gay porn star is Brent Corrigan."

"Yeah . . . I know of him," I said, glancing over to Jessica, who was sitting on the other side of John and eagerly discussing something with Christina.

"He really turns me on," said John. There was something in his eye that made me nervous, though I couldn't quite put my finger on what it was.

Everything happened very quickly after that. John leaned in close and pushed his tongue into my mouth, and before I knew what was happening, he was full on making out with me. For a moment, I was completely paralyzed, but then I decided to play along. The man isn't exactly ugly, after all, and it was a long time since I last kissed anyone.

But as John and I made out, I kept glancing over to Jessica, who was staring at us, frozen. She blushed when our eyes met, and quickly covered her face with her brunette hair (she was brunette at the time).

> *"They love to tell you stay inside the lines, but something's better on the other side."*
> —John Mayer

After that, she sat with her head bowed and began massaging his dick with one hand. John groaned quietly as he kissed me, but I was just trying to work out what was going on.

Not long after, he leaned back on the couch with a satisfied look on his face. He turned and gazed affectionately at Jessica, who didn't seem to know whether she was incredibly embarrassed or really turned on.

I felt like the situation demanded another drink, so I waved the waitress over and got a vodka Red Bull, which used to be my drink of choice. I woke up the next day with such a surreal feeling that I had to look at myself in the hotel mirror and ask, "Did that really happen?"

It was around this time that I first started to earn a serious amount of money, mostly because I had become an attractive proposition for a whole bunch of brands. I even managed to find sponsors for my birthday party at the Roxy in West Hollywood.

It was a fantastic evening, and I gave it the name "the Queen's Birthday Ball." I'd invited several hundred people, and I treated them all to champagne and cupcakes from the famous Sprinkles bakery in Beverly Hills. I even put on live music for them. Among the bands performing (for me!) were UltraViolet Sound and, fittingly, the Gossip. I even got burlesque queen Dita Von Teese, who had recently separated from Marilyn Manson, to give us a spectacular closing number.

Some of the guests were already friends of mine—John Stamos, Kelly Osbourne, and Amy Winehouse—but others were people I was meeting for the first time. Katy Perry was one of the latter, and when I welcomed her in, she laughed a little and complimented my unusual bright-blue hair color. I knew right away that I loved her.

As UltraViolet Sound began to play, I watched as she became transfixed by the music, and I recognized myself in that. Katy and

I became good friends, and she invited me to her own birthday party on the Sunset Strip the following year. Sadly, we lost touch when she became Katy Perry to the whole world, and I had to report not only on things that happened in her professional life, but in her marriage to Russell Brand, too. If she hadn't become such a big star, I actually think we'd still be friends.

I really went mainstream in 2007, and one of the main indicators was the fact that VH1 asked me to make a series of specials for them. Another sign was that I had no trouble booking artists like Dolly Parton, Pink, Janet Jackson, Nelly Furtado, and Gloria Estefan to the show.

I was the tastemaker, the artist breaker. I was living the dream. But, like always when everything seems to be going your way, I was actually just a hair's breadth from ruin.

16

Radio Perez

I am the American dream my parents left Cuba for.

For three years, I had handled everything that had to do with PerezHilton.com by myself, but when I flew to Australia to host the red carpet and present at the MTV Australia Awards in 2007, I got pneumonia and spent most of my time there in bed with a fever. A doctor actually came out to see me in my hotel suite, and by the end of the week more visits followed—I was in such pain all over my body.

Somehow, miraculously, I still managed my hosting duties. I also managed the club appearance I had been booked to do—even if I was in a hospital bed as I hosted the party. I was exhausted, plain and simple, and it suddenly dawned on me that I needed help.

So, when I got back to L.A., I called my mom and sister and asked whether they might be interested in working for me. It was scary at first, because my sister is the opposite of me in every sense. Where I'm creative, she's more business-minded, and I was afraid we would spend all our time fighting. Thankfully, I quickly realized we actually complemented one another perfectly and that she was a great employee who always stayed on top of things. I also knew that I could always trust her.

It was around this time that I stopped working out of the Coffee Bean & Tea Leaf and got myself a two-bedroom apartment with a loft instead. It was actually the same apartment complex where they filmed *The Hills*, but they had already moved out by the time I arrived.

I got my mom and my sister their own apartment on the floor below, and hired a bunch of tradesmen to decorate the place, turning my second bedroom into a closet for all my clothes. We stayed there until I had enough money to buy a place of my own and rent an apartment across the street for my mom and sister.

———

Around this time, the tone of my website went from bitchy to downright nasty. The more snarky names I gave the celebrities, the more penises or coke and boogers I drew on pictures of them, the more people visited my page. By this point I was getting between seven and eight million unique hits a day.

When Britney Spears was at her wildest, people were glued to my website. They were constantly refreshing the page to read the latest news about her, because there was always so much going on. She would drive around in her car for hours with helicopters full of paparazzi following her everywhere. That's how wild it was.

Over the years, I've often been asked how I managed to break so many stories, and the answer is simple: I quickly built up a huge network of contacts. Take the time Lindsay Lohan fled the scene after she crashed her car on Robertson Boulevard, for example. I got a call from one of my friends who worked on that street, and he took photos for me.

For a long time Lindsay was considered damaged goods.

I've often been asked how I managed to break so many stories, and the answer is simple: I quickly built up a huge network of contacts.

A lot of people probably still think of her that way. But in 2007, everything really did go to shit for her. I mean, she was dropped by almost everyone who worked with her. The only person who really cared about her was talent manager Larry Rudolph (currently Britney's manager). He wasn't working with her in any official capacity at the time, but more out of the goodness of his own heart, one day he called me up and said, "I really want you to try to talk to Lindsay."

"Why me?" I asked. I was a little surprised, because although Lindsay and I were on friendly terms, I was constantly writing about everything she did. That spring, for example, she was in a same-sex relationship with DJ Samantha Ronson, who later sued me for defamation and lost. Despite that, Larry seemed to think I was the right person to talk to her. So although I was hesitant, I said, "OK, so take her over to my mom's place." I didn't want the paparazzi that followed her everywhere to know where I lived.

"Thank you," said Larry. He really did sound relieved. "Can we come over this afternoon?"

Just a few hours later, we met at Mom's place across the street from my house. Lindsay was at rock bottom, and I don't know whether it helped or not, but I listened to what she had to say; I gave her advice and did what I could to help get her back on the right track.

The fact that managers sometimes got in touch to give me tips about their own stars wasn't actually that unusual. In fact, to this day I still have people I can talk to in Britney's camp. Back then, I actually had two, one of whom was her shady manager at the time, Sam Lutfi. He was constantly getting in touch. If I can be crass for a moment, I think he did it because he was a star fucker, and I had the advantage of not only being a celebrity blogger but a celebrity in my own right. People like him were desperate to give me information.

Of course, I also found out about a lot of stories myself, at the events I invited myself to. There were times when I was ejected from things—not everyone wanted me there, and I'm actually still banned from the Chateau Marmont in West Hollywood. But I didn't care, even if the way I found out about it was a little strange. I had been invited to a party at the hotel by an agency I was a client of, but when I got there, one of the staff pulled me to one side and said, "You have to leave."

I remember I had no idea what was going on. "Why?" I asked, holding up my hands.

"You're not welcome here."

A few years later, I was dating a guy, and he announced one day that he had a surprise for me. It wasn't until we were

approaching the hotel that he revealed he'd booked us a staycation at the Chateau.

"I'm sorry," I said, "but I don't think I'm welcome there."

The guy just laughed and said, "Nah, it'll be fine, that was so long ago."

"OK," I said, "but give them a call first, just to double-check."

He did as I said, and I heard the receptionist's voice clearly down the line, "No, Perez Hilton is not permitted to be here."

―――――――

I was being sued constantly; it was also something I simply got used to. Multiple photo agencies sued me for using their photos without permission. Britney's record label sued me for leaking her new album, and Jennifer Aniston sued me for posting a leaked topless image cut from a movie. The image never made it into the actual film, and what I posted was a scan of the French newspaper that published it first. Though I got sued, they didn't.

During these years, I made sure to be as active as I could on my various platforms (I still am), and I obsessively checked Twitter for replies so that I could like every single one. It was a way for me to show my followers that I read what they wrote, but that didn't necessarily mean I liked it all.

It was around this time that I also ran into Jesse Metcalfe, one of the actors from *Desperate Housewives*, at an event. Like *Glee* a few years later, that show was a cultural phenomenon. Looking back now, I don't actually remember what I wrote about him, but it must have been bad enough to make him mad, because with a stony face he turned to me and said, "Do you know how many times I've fantasized about killing you?"

Roseanne Barr said something similar. Something about wanting to kidnap me and take me to her farm in Hawaii so she could say I was trespassing and then shoot me. But I didn't care. That was partly down to being young and believing I would be successful forever, but it was also because I thought I was happy.

In reality, I was drowning in negativity. I was stuck playing a part, too afraid to change, too afraid of losing my readers if I suddenly stopped being so mean. In a professional sense, things were going better than ever, and on May 5, 2008, my nationally syndicated radio show, *Radio Perez*, which included updates from my blog, would premiere. In order to be able to call in to New York and Chicago radio, I had to get up early and rarely got more than four or five hours' sleep a night. That went on for a long time. Nine years, to be precise.

17

Circus

I mock and heckle a pop star with mental health issues,
and am later asked to join her tour.

Britney Spears is probably the person I've spent the most time writing and talking about over the years, partly because of her huge fame and her ability to repeatedly cause problems for herself.

Her downfall had begun in January 2004, when she married Jason Alexander, a childhood friend from Kentwood, Louisiana. She invited him to Las Vegas, and Jason seems to have assumed that she just wanted company and a good time, but when he got there, Britney suddenly said, "Let's get married."

So, that's what they did, at the Little White Chapel. The marriage was annulled fifty-five hours later because, according to the paperwork, Britney "lacked understanding of her actions, to the extent that she was incapable of agreeing to the marriage."

The craziness continued after that, culminating in 2007, her dark, monster year. The year had barely begun before she checked into a rehab center in Antigua for less than twenty-four hours, shaving all her hair off with a pair of clippers at a hair salon in Tarzana, Los Angeles, the very next night.

She continued to check in and out of rehab in the months that followed, was reported to the cops for a hit and run, and had a breakdown when her ex-husband, Kevin Federline, sought sole custody of their two sons (a request that was ultimately granted by the courts). Despite that, I still nursed some kind of hope that she would pull herself

I still nursed some kind of hope that she would pull herself together.

together and be on the lookout for revenge at the 2007 MTV Video Music Awards in Las Vegas—her first time on stage in three years.

I was there, and I'd received some slightly worrying reports that she had gone out clubbing rather than rehearsing or resting. But since I really liked her, I didn't want to believe things were as bad as people said. As it happens, they weren't—they were far worse.

The minute she came out onstage to open the show with her new single, "Gimme More," I was shocked. She looked unhealthy, unkempt, and uncomfortable in her skimpy costume, and she seemed to be moving awkwardly. But the worst part was that she completely failed to lip-sync properly, and actually forgot the words midsong, giving up at one point. It was so bad that I could hardly believe what I was seeing and hearing. That's why I didn't try to soften the blow: I wrote that she should be ashamed of herself, that she was an embarrassment—something I really regret today.

At the same time, I don't think anyone really understood the extent of her problems. I know I didn't, in any case; like many others, I just assumed that her meltdown was a result of her wild party lifestyle and all the drugs she was taking. It never occurred to me that there might be some kind of mental health issue behind her behavior. Looking back now, it really does seem like Britney is lucky to still be alive.

In early 2008, when Britney was admitted to a psychiatric hospital, it became clear to everyone where her problems stemmed from—but obviously I couldn't take back everything I'd written.

That's why, in January 2009, I was surprised to get a call from Jamie King, who said, "Hey, do you want to be a part of Britney's big comeback tour?" Jamie was a choreographer and director, and he'd worked with stars like Prince, Madonna, Ricky Martin, and the Spice Girls. He had also worked on Britney's Oops! . . . I Did It Again tour eight years earlier.

"Uhh . . ." I said, trying to gather my thoughts. My mind was racing. "That sounds awesome, but I need to know whether this is Britney's idea or yours."

"It was my idea," Jamie replied, sounding cheery.

I cleared my throat. "So is Britney OK with this?"

"Yeah," he said. "She's already approved it. She's really excited to have you play a part in her show."

"Really?" I couldn't quite hide the skepticism in my voice, but obviously I was also flattered.

Jamie explained that he wanted me to play the main part in the video they would show at the start of every concert during the tour, which had been given the name Circus.

"Aha," I said. "So who, or what, would I be playing?"

"The Mean Queen."

I had absolutely nothing against that, and when the time came to shoot the video, I realized that it was heavily based on the Queen of Hearts from *Alice's Adventures in Wonderland*.

Once my makeup was done and I got into my costume, it was so great to see the final result in the mirror. And as I went out onstage in front of the cameras to introduce Britney to the audience, I also got to put my acting skills to use for once.

Britney herself didn't take part in the recording, which ended with a look-alike coming out into the

> ## *"You'll Never See It My Way, Because You're Not Me!"*
> —Britney Spears

circus ring with a crossbow and shooting me—thankfully they missed, letting me live.

It wasn't until a year later that I actually met her, at a Grammy Awards party. I remember I went up to her and introduced myself, and she was super friendly—though I also had a strong sense that she had no idea who I was.

2008

BRITNEY SPEARS LOSES VISITATION RIGHTS AFTER REFUSING TO TURN OVER HER SONS TO HER EX-HUSBAND.

HEATH LEDGER IS FOUND DEAD AT AGE TWENTY-EIGHT.

NAOMI CAMPBELL PLEADS GUILTY TO ASSAULTING TWO POLICE OFFICERS.

HEATHER LOCKLEAR IS CHARGED WITH DRIVING UNDER THE INFLUENCE.

18

Peak Perez

My career goes from strength to strength, but I haven't slept with anyone in over a year.

It was New Year's Eve, and I should have been happy. It had been an incredible year—2007 had essentially been the golden year of celebrity gossip. America had woken up to a new scandal practically every day, and I'd had a record number of visitors on my website.

I still didn't have much competition; there just weren't many other websites like mine, and social media was still a relatively new phenomenon. In many respects, I was as famous as the people I was writing about, and for the second year in a row I had been booked to host MTV's live New Year's show from Times Square.

To put it bluntly, my career was at its peak, though on an emotional level I was somewhere else entirely as I checked into the W Hotel, right by MTV Studios.

Like the year before, 2007 had been a great success professionally, but in terms of my private life, it had been a complete disaster. I felt more lost than ever, but above all I was lonely, and I had been comfort eating in an attempt to dampen the sadness for longer than I wanted to admit. The result, of course, was that I had put on a lot of weight, and I had also begun to develop a real complex about how I looked. It meant I didn't want to get undressed in front of anyone, and I hadn't had sex even once over the past year—for a gay man, that's practically unheard of.

In a desperate attempt to hide how little I liked myself, I had begun experimenting with different—but all more or less crazy—hair colors: pink, banana yellow, silver, black, blond, purple, magenta, clear blue. . . . And as I checked my reflection in the mirror in my little hotel room before heading to the party,

I remember wishing that I could press a button and go up in a cloud of smoke.

I remember wishing that I could press a button and go up in a cloud of smoke.

The man I saw looked bloated, with an eggplant-color emo haircut and a shimmering mask of make up around his sad eyes. Truly, I looked like a faded clown, and though MTV had asked me to host their New Year's party—a fact that should have been clear proof I was doing something right—I felt like complete crap.

"Get it together," I told the clown in the mirror. "You have a job to do—a job other people would die for." Not long after, as I approached the red carpet, I actually found myself enjoying the excitement I was creating.

During the previous few weeks, my cohost Tila Tequila (a MySpace personality and *Playboy* model turned reality star) and I had been throwing shit at one another in interviews, meaning we had the worst ever chemistry for two hosts. I have a suspicion that was what MTV was hoping for, but either way it was the reason the photographers were swarming around me like wasps around a trashcan. That suited me perfectly, not least because it allowed me to forget myself for a while.

As for the party, there isn't much to say other than it all went well, though the production team did occasionally have to physically pull Tila and me apart.

But once I got back to my hotel room, I felt worse than I had before I left. I remember taking off my velvet jacket, kicking off my shoes, and then heading straight for the tiny desk, where there was an ice bucket and a bottle of champagne waiting for me. I read the New Year's greeting from MTV on the card and popped the cork. I didn't actually like champagne all that much, but this was one of those occasions when I felt like not only was it justified to use any means necessary to chase my demons, but I actually didn't have any choice.

I filled a glass and sat down on my bed to look out of the window. Every now and again, fireworks lit up the sky, and I could still hear the party going on in Times Square. I swigged my champagne and tried to feel some kind of satisfaction, but it was impossible. It was like I was racing myself, methodically emptying the bottle by constantly topping up my glass. The carousel had temporarily stopped, and the noise had been replaced by complete nothingness.

I raised the glass and toasted myself. But if I had been hoping to cheer myself up with the gesture, it left me feeling even more downbeat.

I need to make some changes, I said to myself.

I really meant it.

19

My Wifey

Lady Gaga and I get to know one another by playing Ping-Pong and voguing to Madonna all night.

I decided to get in shape in January 2008, setting myself up for success by treating myself as though I were a drug addict. In other words, I didn't just go cold turkey, I started making small changes to my eating habits. That was how I began to lose weight.

It wasn't easy, because I had been a big eater since I was a kid. Since I was making progress, I decided to start walking more regularly after a month or so. Not every day, and not for too long—something like thirty minutes five times a week. That meant I lost even more weight, which motivated me to join a gym, hire a personal trainer, and start doing two workout sessions a day.

At around the same time, I started getting emails from someone claiming to be an assistant for Troy Carter, a music manager. Troy would go on to enjoy huge success with a number of established stars, but at the time he was managing an unknown artist named Lady Gaga, who was busy working on her debut album.

Troy's assistant asked whether I would be interested in listening to a few of her tracks, ending one email with "She's amazing." It wasn't exactly the first time I had heard management say something like that, but I decided to give her a chance and wrote a quick "Sure" back.

Two seconds later, I heard the email ping into my inbox, and to make sure I wouldn't forget about it, I listened to the track right away. I was completely floored. The assistant had—maybe without even really knowing it—been telling the truth.

I shared *Just Dance* with my readers as soon as it came out. What you need to remember is that streaming music platforms hadn't really caught on yet in 2008, and Twitter still hadn't had its big breakthrough. All in all, that meant it was harder to get your music out there, so the fact that I posted her track to my website, which had millions of visitors a day, was a big deal. I remember writing something along the lines of "She reminds me so much of Madonna."

Later that spring, I contacted Lady Gaga's management team to ask if she could perform at the Fourth of July party I was hosting at Planet Hollywood in Las Vegas. I explained that there was no money in it, but that the gig was guaranteed to sell out.

They said yes almost immediately, so I called a friend of mine, the publicist at the now-closed Privé club in Vegas, and said, "Is it OK if I book a performer?" There was silence on the other end of the line, but before she had time to argue, I quickly added, "I want this girl called Lady Gaga to perform, and she'll do it for free."

That seemed to ease any doubts she might have had, because all she said was "Sure."

———————

When I arrived in Vegas a few weeks later, I had really high hopes for the gig. First because I was so impressed by the track I'd heard, but also because she had sounded super sweet when we talked on the phone.

I had also begun to promote her on my website, and the reaction so far told me my instincts had been right: Lady Gaga was not your average pop star. As I checked in to Planet Hollywood, I felt genuinely happy for the first time in a long while.

I had only just gotten to my suite and slumped onto the bed when my phone beeped. A few friends had just arrived in town, and they were pumped for the evening.

Not long after, I also got a message from Lady Gaga, who wrote that she was in a car on her way to the hotel. I replied that I had booked a table at a restaurant before the club performance. I took a shower and fixed myself up before meeting my friends to head to the restaurant.

We had just sat down when Gaga arrived. I'll never forget the way she seemed to be glowing. There are certain people you feel like you've known for a long time from the moment you meet them, and that's exactly how it was with Gaga.

I introduced myself, and she said that not only did she know who I was, she was also a big fan of mine.

"Really?" I asked.

She laughed. "Yeah, I check your website several times a day."

Gaga thanked me for promoting her, and I thanked her for agreeing to perform for free at my party. Looking back now, it probably seems like we were using one another—but not in a bad way. In fact, I felt like we were lucky to have met at the exact right moment.

The Fourth of July party was a hit—not least thanks to Gaga. I remember being really impressed by her performance. Donnie Wahlberg, from the New Kids on the Block, clearly agreed, because he later said that the Vegas gig was where he first saw her, and that it was the main reason he booked Gaga as the support act on NKOTB's reunion tour.

In any case, once the gig was over, we were all having so much fun that we didn't want the night to end, so we continued the party in my suite playing Ping-Pong and voguing to Madonna into the early hours.

I continued to promote Gaga on my website and made sure to take her to a whole bunch of events. Before long, it felt like we were genuinely close. We would spend hours talking on the phone almost every day. She asked me what I thought about various ideas; I told her, and I gave her ideas in return. The whole thing was intoxicating and exciting. She valued my opinions and talked to me like I was part of the team, like a close friend.

"Do you know the feeling of your heart being so terribly broken you can feel the blood dripping out?"

—Lady Gaga

One of the events I had her perform at was the CMJ party in New York. It's a music festival that has taken place every October since 1980, involving both open seminars and live performances. Gaga's company made the whole thing not only bearable but actually fun.

We always had a lot of fun, and started hanging out practically all the time. We even began celebrating holidays together, and after a while, I jokingly started calling her my "wifey."

But as my relationship with Gaga deepened, she was becoming a phenomenon, enjoying huge success all over the world. The hit records followed one after another, and she suddenly found herself heading off on huge tours.

Gaga always wanted me to tag along, and I thought it was incredible—partly because I got to hang out with someone who had become one of my closest friends, but also because I got to see parts of America and the rest of the world that I had never visited before. It was cool to fly to Australia on a promo tour, for example. Not to mention Tokyo—that was probably the best of our trips together. We went to karaoke bars and gay clubs every night, plus completely ordinary bars that felt anything but ordinary purely because they were in Japan.

At this point, she was still just a young girl, and she didn't drink any more or less than most others her age. But before long—as she became LADY GAGA to the world—she began drinking in a different, more serious way, while also popping all kinds of pills. I saw it happening but said nothing, because I knew how difficult it was to deal with the chaos all around her.

What I did instead was to protect her as best I could, always taking her side—even if that meant hurting others. I even went as far as to deliberately hurt Christina Aguilera just a few months after she had been kind enough to perform at my birthday party. Why? Because Gaga and I thought Christina was copying her with the sound of her new album, *Bionic*, and the visuals during that era.

I started giving Christina all kinds of terrible nicknames on my website. Looking back now, it's one of the things I'm most ashamed of, and I can also see that Gaga was using me as a tool—not only against Christina but against her other rivals too. She never explicitly asked me to write nasty things about people, but by moaning to me she made me feel like I, her best friend, should do something about it.

Gaga was using me as a tool — not only against Christina but against her other rivals too.

On the one hand, she used me as a kind of human torpedo to guarantee better press coverage, but on the other, she asked for advice and genuinely valued my opinion on music and business. She also confided in me and gave me recognition. I can remember countless occasions when she told other people, "If it wasn't for Perez, I wouldn't be here today."

She was also there for me when I was having a tough time, like later that year when my then boyfriend dumped me. The minute Gaga heard about it, she called me and said, "You can't be alone right now, meet me in Detroit."

I flew over there the very next day, and the tears began flowing the minute I saw her. She comforted me and said, "OK, we're doing something fun."

She probably realized that in my broken state, I didn't need alcohol, so instead of taking me to a bar, we went to a bowling alley, where we bumped into Meg White of the White Stripes. Before long, we were having the kind of fun that only Gaga and I could.

2009

ROMAN POLANSKI IS ARRESTED IN ZURICH, THIRTY YEARS AFTER PLEADING GUILTY TO HAVING SEX WITH A THIRTEEN-YEAR-OLD GIRL IN L.A. AND THEN FLEEING JUSTICE.

CHRIS BROWN ATTACKS RIHANNA.

MICHAEL JACKSON DIES.

DAVID LETTERMAN CONFESSES TO HAVING SEX WITH MEMBERS OF HIS STAFF.

TIGER WOODS CHEATS ON HIS WIFE, ELIN NORDEGREN.

JUSTIN BIEBER COMES TO MY HOUSE TO PERFORM FOR MY YOUTUBE CHANNEL.

20

Miss USA

I insult a beauty queen and become an It Girl myself.

In April 2009, when I was asked to be a judge on the Miss USA pageant, I felt honored. Not just because the pageant was a big deal in the United States, but because I had always loved watching it on TV. The show would be broadcast live from Planet Hollywood in Las Vegas—the same hotel I had been staying at the summer before, when I met Lady Gaga for the first time.

I remember I arrived the day before the pageant so I could be there for the rehearsals and so I could attend the premiere of *Peepshow*, a lavish burlesque show starring Mel B from the Spice Girls. The show was right up my street, and I spent half the night afterward partying with Mel, Holly Madison, and Lindsay Lohan. But the very next day, it was time to get to work. I was wearing a green jacket, and in the briefing meeting—where they show you how the voting apparatus works, and that kind of thing—I found out that I would be allowed to ask a question during the question and answer section. The producers had told us that we could either write a question ourselves, or else they would come up with one for us.

I decided, "I'm gonna write my own question!"

I remember thinking about what I could ask that would not only be a good question but also bring attention to the show and get people talking about me. You have to remember that in 2009, Barack Obama had only just been elected president. That was a great high, but the LGBT community had suffered a big setback at the same time, when Proposition 8 passed in California, making it illegal for same-sex couples to marry. Similar things had begun happening in a lot of other states, too, so I came up with what I thought was a very timely and relevant question to ask.

At this point in the competition, one of the remaining contestants was Miss Utah, and I really wanted to put my question to her. As you may know, there are more Mormons in Utah than anywhere else on earth, and the Mormon Church had donated a lot of money in support of Proposition 8. They backed hatred, to put it bluntly, and I wanted to demonstrate that to the American people.

Sadly, to my disappointment, it was Miss California who pulled the piece of paper with my name on it from the glass bowl onstage.

Oh, man, I thought. *This is gonna be a breeze*. In my mind, the question of same-sex marriage shouldn't be the least bit controversial to a young woman from California.

I grabbed the mic, looked up at Miss California, and said, "Vermont recently became the fourth state to legalize same-sex marriage. Do you think every state should follow suit? Why or why not?"

"Well, I think it's great that Americans are able to choose one or the other," she replied. "We live in a land where you can choose same-sex marriage or opposite marriage."

Opposite marriage? I thought. *What the hell does she mean by that?*

But I didn't need to ask, because she went on, "You know what, in my country, and in my family, I think I believe that a

I grabbed the mic, looked up at Miss California, and said, "Vermont recently became the fourth state to legalize same-sex marriage. Do you think every state should follow suit? Why or why not?"

marriage should be between a man and a woman. No offense to anybody out there, but that's how I was raised and that's how I think it should be. Thank you."

If I hadn't been so shocked, I probably would have raised the mic to my lips and pointed out that she was free *not* to choose same-sex marriage. But she just smiled and seemed deadly serious about what she said. She also seemed completely oblivious to the fact that she had just ignited a firestorm, partly because same-sex marriage was such a hot-button issue in America at the time, and partly because it was the perfect question to be asked by the perfect person at the perfect time. I was an openly gay man who was directly affected by the prejudice and hostility of bigoted idiots like her.

Fortunately, she wasn't crowned Miss USA, and I like to think that's partly because I showed her up. The minute the broadcast was over, I went back up to my room. By that point, the shock at what she had said had been replaced by so much anger that I was shaking, and before I knew what I was doing, I was on my laptop, recording a video for my website.

I was still wearing my green jacket, and began by saying that Miss California had just given the worst answer in pageant history. I really ramped it up after that, saying, "She didn't lose because she doesn't believe in gay marriage. Miss California lost because she's a dumb bitch!"

Once I'd gotten that out of me, I calmed my nerves with a cocktail in one of the hotel bars and met up with my Las Vegas besties, Mike and Alex.

When I woke up the next morning, I realized that my video had instantly become a huge political thing, and that *everyone* seemed to be talking about me and what I'd said. I could hardly believe it. It was like Christmas had come early, and it didn't take long for all the TV and radio stations to start getting in touch.

Over the weeks that followed, I did so many media appearances that I lost count. I appeared on *Larry King Live*, for example, and I'm sure I surprised a lot of his audience by being both informed and a good advocate of same-sex marriage. Hopefully I managed to change a few hearts and minds that day.

———

A few years later, I was asked if I wanted be a judge on the Miss Universe pageant, which was being broadcast from the same hotel in Vegas.

Like before, I had the chance to ask one of the participants a question, and I came up with something I thought might spark debate. But when the broadcast eventually came around, and it was time to ask my question, something unexpected happened. During some introductory chat with one of the hosts, I was asked what I thought the difference was between Miss USA and Miss Universe.

I answered honestly, with the first thing that came to mind: "Well, the two big differences are, number one, a lot more people watch Miss Universe and, number two, thankfully Donald Trump no longer owns this pageant."

The audience began laughing, but the host looked completely shocked, like she didn't know what to say. After that, no one really cared about my question—particularly not after what happened next.

There were just two finalists still standing, Miss Colombia and Miss Philippines, and they were both waiting nervously on the stage, holding hands. Steve Harvey (the main host) shouted, "Miss Universe 2015 is . . . Colombia!"

The other judges and I stared at one another in confusion. Though we weren't supposed to discuss who we were voting for, we obviously had, and we knew that most of us had voted for Miss Philippines—purely because she had given the best answers and seemed the most humble of the two.

Miss Colombia was handed flowers and a crown, and the audience began cheering, but Steve came back out onstage, looking like he wanted the ground to swallow him up. With his head bowed, he moved over to Miss Colombia, who was now an incredibly happy Miss Universe, and mumbled into the microphone, "Okay, folks . . . uhm . . . I have to apologize . . . "

The audience, who had worked out what was going on, began to shout, and Miss Colombia's smile stiffened. Steve held up a large card and began reading from it, explaining that he had made a terrible mistake.

Eventually he said, "Miss Universe 2015 is Philippines!"

Yet again, the judges stared at one another, trying to work out what the hell was going on. Miss Philippines herself seemed to be struggling to understand.

Everything got even wilder after that, because we suddenly found out that the theater was on lockdown due to rumors of a shooting outside. People were still going crazy over the mistake, but now some madman was shooting at random? I remember my jaw literally dropped.

As it happened, it wasn't a shooting at all, but something crazy *did* happen. A mentally unstable woman had run over people with her car on the strip outside the theater, so there was all kinds of craziness going on, inside and out.

Whether I wanted it or not, clearly I couldn't be a judge on a beauty pageant without complete chaos breaking loose.

2010–2011

CHRISTINA AGUILERA IS BRIEFLY ARRESTED AFTER BEING FOUND DRUNK IN PUBLIC AND DEEMED UNABLE TO TAKE CARE OF HERSELF.

RYAN REYNOLDS LEAVES SCARLETT JOHANSSON FOR SANDRA BULLOCK.

CHARLIE SHEEN TRASHES HIS HOTEL ROOM AND RUNS AROUND NAKED AFTER PARTYING WITH AN ESCORT IN NEW YORK CITY.

A FEW MONTHS LATER, SHEEN'S EX-WIFE BROOKE MUELLER FILES A RESTRAINING ORDER AGAINST HIM, PROHIBITING HIM FROM BEING WITHIN A HUNDRED YARDS OF HER, AND THE POLICE TEMPORARILY TAKE HIS TWIN BOYS OUT OF HIS CUSTODY.

IT EMERGES THAT ARNOLD SCHWARZENEGGER HAS A LOVE CHILD FROM AN AFFAIR WITH HIS FORMER HOUSEKEEPER, MILDRED BAENA.

21

Love Is a Dog from Hell

My boyfriend turns to his guru to make me over.

I don't think I've ever been in love. I've been in two relationships, the longest of which lasted a year, and I know that I *thought* I was in love. But looking back now, I'm not so sure. I think I was just excited that someone seemed to want me.

The man—let's call him Craig—was actually too young for me. Yes, he was twenty-five, but he was also inexperienced, and when we met on a gay dating website called Connexion in 2010, he had only ever been with one other guy—ever.

Anyone in my situation would have been a little skeptical, and I actually remember saying to him, "Are you sure you don't want to sleep around a little before you settle down in a relationship?"

But Craig looked me straight in the eye and said, "No, absolutely not. I know I've found the right guy now, and I want to be with you—not someone else."

"OK, good," I said, trying to feel as genuinely happy as I knew I should in that moment, now that I had a boyfriend.

But there was a tiny nugget of doubt left in me, and whenever it rose to the surface, I felt guilty, like I was being unfair. Because the truth is that Craig really did like me, and he demonstrated that in a number of ways.

What he didn't like was my job. That hurt me, and though I tried to ignore it, it was always there between us, like some kind of unspoken obstacle.

Fortunately, we had great chemistry—in terms of sex, that is—and I found him interesting because he was so different from me. Above all, he had a spiritual side that came out in a number of ways. When we were at home, for example, he often had his nose buried in a self-help book, and he would come over to me where I was working and talk about the meaning of life, mankind's untapped abilities, and a holy, universal power that affected everything. It was a pretty stark contrast to whatever I was focused on in that moment.

Sometimes this irritated me, and I didn't know what to say. But more often than not, I actually found it stimulating that he asked questions about our existence. Above all, I loved how serious he was. I found it kind of touching.

It probably wasn't surprising that Craig had a life coach whom he saw regularly for advice. He had met her in Hawaii, and claimed she had changed his life. I didn't know quite what to believe, but I didn't say anything—partly out of respect and partly because I didn't want to get into a discussion that might go on forever.

But one afternoon, he came in to my home office and said, "I think you should meet her."

"Who?" I asked, only half listening.

"My life coach," said Craig.

"Huh?" I said, turning to him.

"I think it would do you good," he told me, smiling what almost looked like a blessed smile. In reality, it was because he wanted to change me, but I didn't realize that at the time.

"OK . . ." I said, and the very next day we headed over to her house.

The first thing I noticed as I stepped through the door was the smoky smell, which made me feel nauseous. Next thing I knew, the woman was standing right in front of us in the faintly lit room.

She greeted me with a big, cold hand, gave me an intense look, and told me to sit down on the cushions on the floor in the next room. I did as she said, but I have to confess I felt anything but relaxed—even though Craig was sitting close by.

"We need to clear the karma from the past." She closed her eyes and held out her palms as she sat cross-legged opposite me. "A pain that needs to be released."

I didn't know what she was talking about, but I didn't say anything. After all, I was there for Craig's sake. I glanced over to him and almost felt shocked when I saw how satisfied he looked.

"Events from your childhood have had a very negative effect on you," the woman continued in a kind of chanting tone, scrunching up her wrinkled face. Her eyes suddenly opened, and she stared at me, making me jump. "But I am going to free you from that pain." She smiled and lowered her hands.

"Before our next session, I want you to take a hot bath and relax, retreat into yourself. Once you feel like you've made contact with your inner child, I want you to write down what the greatest trauma of your childhood is."

"In the bath?" I asked.

She nodded and then said, "Your inner child will guide your hand, and when we meet we'll go through what you wrote."

I thought it sounded *really* lame, but again I kept my doubts to myself. I didn't even say anything to Craig on the way home. But we had barely made it into the house when he turned to me and said, "I guess you might as well take a bath now?" To say he sounded keen would be an understatement.

"I think I'll do it tomorrow, after I go to the gym," I said, noticing the look of disappointment on his face. I quickly added, "I mean, my body will be relaxed then, so it won't be able to put up any resistance to that inner child."

Craig seemed to accept that explanation, and for the rest of the day he showed me the kind of affection that only ever stems from being obeyed.

As promised, I ran a hot bath the very next day, and as I lay in it I thought about what I had been through in my childhood. I found myself writing down the kind of thing that was expected of me: Dad's death, being bullied at school, eating in front of the TV. The most obvious things, in other words.

But when the guru read what I had scrawled down—on a piece of paper that was completely crinkled from the steam—she seemed so happy, and said, "Excellent. Now we can free you from the pain you have been carrying around."

She scrunched the paper into a ball and placed it on top of a couple of dried sage leaves in a metal bowl on the table between us. She then passed me a box of matches.

"Destroy your darkness!"

I stared at her, still a little unsure whether this wasn't all just some joke. But both she and Craig (who had come along again) looked so sincere and encouraging that I thought I may as well do what they wanted.

Before long, I had lit a match and set fire to the ball of paper, which quickly burned up.

The guru clapped her hands and exclaimed, "Bless you, free soul!"

"How does it feel?" Craig asked, giving me a curious glance.

"Uh . . . " I said, frantically searching for the right words. "Like a weight has been lifted from my chest." But in truth, I was thinking, *What a bullshit guru!*

I was thinking, *What a bullshit guru!*

Craig seemed happy, in any case, but it didn't last long. Probably because he quickly realized I had no intention of shutting down my website and finding another way to make a living—a way that he approved of.

That became particularly clear a few weeks later, when I threw a party to celebrate my thirty-second birthday. It was March 2010, and in hindsight, I can easily say it was the best Hollywood party I ever went to. Like always, I organized it in collaboration with DMF Media—I used them for all my parties, and thankfully never had to pay them for the service; it was a working relationship. The whole thing was fun, but it was also an opportunity for me to get my name out there and to help the DMF brand.

That particular year, the party was at Paramount Studios, and everyone who was anyone was there—particularly since the MTV Movie Awards had been filmed nearby that same day. My party became the unofficial after-party for the awards.

Justin Bieber was there, Lindsay Lohan was there, John Stamos, too. Everyone I knew or had a relationship with. I'd thrown legendary birthday parties before, including one I called the Blue Ball, where everyone dressed in blue and a handful of megastars performed. Selena Gomez sang "Happy Birthday," for example. The party in 2010 was no different, and I had the most iconic, eclectic, phenomenal lineup. Liza Minnelli and Leona Lewis both performed for free, and Katy Perry surprised me by showing up on an elephant to sing "Happy Birthday." It was the same elephant she used in the "Waking Up in Vegas" video.

I was dressed to the nines in a custom gold lamé suit, but on the inside I felt really sad. Craig was my date, but he kept his distance all night, and before long I realized that he didn't want to be seen with me. If the same happened now, I'd talk to my boyfriend about what was going on, or at least handle the situation differently. But in that particular relationship, I was pretty pussy-whipped. I almost felt like I was walking on eggshells around him. I tried so hard to save our relationship that maybe I actually smothered him.

For Valentine's Day a few weeks earlier, I had booked a hotel room in Santa Mnica. Throughout our relationship, I'd given him little gifts or letters every day, to show him how much he meant to me. One week, for example, I gave him a recipe book and said we could use it to cook together. Another week, I gave him a snow globe and wrote "I wanna share my world with you." My submissiveness was probably down to the fact that I couldn't believe someone as handsome and smart as him could be interested in a guy like me, and just a few weeks later, as we were eating dinner, he turned to me and said, "I'm sorry, but this isn't working." I had suspected something like that was coming, so I wasn't particularly surprised.

22

The Change

I get punched in the face and have a change of heart.

Aside from giving celebrities awful nicknames and mocking and drawing dicks on pictures of them, I often also outed them and published pictures of their kids. It was like I had distanced myself not only from Mario Lavandeira but also from the celebrities themselves, and I treated them more like characters in a soap opera than real people.

The wake-up was painful, and it all started at Universal's after-party for the Much Music Video Awards in Toronto in 2010, when I got into an argument with will.i.am—and got punched.

When I came around, I couldn't work out what had just happened. Someone helped me to my feet, and I learned that will.i.am's manager had just punched me. When I lifted my hand to my face, I felt a sharp pain. Tears welled up in my eyes. It wasn't just that I was in shock; I felt humiliated somehow, in a way I hadn't since I was at school.

This was also the year I published an up-skirt shot of a seventeen-year-old Miley Cyrus. She was wearing underwear, but it was still an up-skirt shot, and she was underage.

We got into a huge fight over that picture when I randomly ran into her at the ArcLight Theater that spring. I had just finished taking pictures by the red carpet when she suddenly appeared in front of me in the lobby.

"What the fuck were you thinking?" she shouted, making everyone around us turn and stare. She continued, telling me exactly what she thought of me and my website, and I replied as best I could.

———

Just a few months later, the news reached me that a gay Rutgers University student named Tyler Clementi had jumped off the George Washington Bridge after his roommate secretly filmed him kissing another man in their dorm. Within the space of just a few weeks, another four teenagers committed suicide after being bullied because of their sexuality. This led journalist Dan Savage to launch an online wellness campaign called It Gets Better, aiming to prevent any further suicides.

I was one of the many people who were shocked by what had happened, and when I recorded a video in support of the campaign, I had no idea what a storm that would kick up.

People wrote such hateful comments that I couldn't bring myself to read even half of them. The strength of the hate storm really shook me, and popped the bubble I had been living in. I realized for the first time that it wasn't just a handful of people who disliked what I did—*it was the overwhelming majority*. I finally understood that the things I wrote genuinely hurt people, and deeply.

The comments called me everything from a hypocrite and a bully to part of the problem, asking how I had the nerve to make my own It Gets Better video when I had outed a whole bunch of famous people myself. That was the

I realized for the first time that it wasn't just a handful of people who disliked what I did — *it was the overwhelming majority*. I finally understood that the things I wrote genuinely hurt people, and deeply.

wake-up call I needed, and just a few days later I made a new video explaining that from that point on, I would be changing the way I wrote about celebrities.

As expected, many people were skeptical about my complete 180 and questioned whether I really meant what I was saying. They thought it was simply an attempt to save my own skin. In the end, I felt like I had no choice but to try to reach out from a bigger platform, so I got in touch with the producers of *The Ellen DeGeneres Show* to ask whether they might have me on as a guest. They said they would call me back, and when they did— later that same day—I got the sense that they'd had to convince Ellen to book me.

Still, in early October I sat down opposite her and tried to explain and defend myself as best I could. I hadn't been allowed to talk to her before the show, and felt a little like I was on trial.

I was super nervous, in other words, but I did at least manage to say what I wanted to say. I have no idea whether she believed me or not, but she did treat me with respect either way.

> *"You get to know who you really are in a crisis."*
> —Oprah Winfrey

Not long after that, someone from Oprah Winfrey's team got in touch. "We've noticed that the way you write has changed. Do you think you'd like to come on with Oprah and talk about that?"

At first, I couldn't say a single word, but I eventually managed to stutter "Yeah." Oprah was someone I had watched throughout my childhood, and I admired her in the same way I admired Madonna.

I was booked to appear on *Oprah's Master Class*, which was filmed live at Radio City Music Hall in New York, and I took my mom and sister with me.

In the days before the interview, I had done everything I could to prepare for her questions. But when I got to the theater and finally saw Oprah, I regressed to being Mario Lavandeira from Westchester—the kid who wrote her letters and prayed for a reply. At the same time, I was my usual honest self. I felt like Oprah really got me, and it didn't take long before she even began finishing my sentences.

That was a huge moment for me, and a vital period of change for the rest of my life.

23

S&M

Madonna, Britney, and Rihanna mess with me.

If Oprah was one of my biggest idols growing up, Madonna was definitely the other, and when I finally met her, I seemed to regress to a child, just like I had with Oprah.

Madonna and I had met in Las Vegas during her Sticky & Sweet tour in November 2008. A few months earlier, her then publicist Liz Rosenberg sent me a short video that Madonna made just for me. I was floored.

I mean, Madonna wasn't just a big inspiration to me—she had been my escape from Miami, from life, and in many respects she was still the ultimate fantasy. That's why I was completely beside myself when a friend called me up

Madonna wasn't just a big inspiration to me—she had been my escape from Miami, from life, and in many respects she was still the ultimate fantasy.

and said, "I got two tickets for Madonna in Vegas and thought we could go."

Two weeks later, we arrived, and as we made our way to the MGM Grand Garden Arena in a cab, I decided to message Liz Rosenberg, who had been Madonna's publicist for over twenty years. I didn't mention anything about wanting to go backstage and meet Madonna, though—partly because it was completely unthinkable that anything like that could happen and partly because I knew Madonna didn't do meet-and-greets before or after her shows. Instead, I just wrote that I was on my way and that I was looking forward to the gig.

My friend and I had only just made it to our seats in the arena when Liz replied, "Hey, where are you? Come meet me. Madonna wants to say hi."

I had to read the message several times. My friend gave me a confused glance. "Come with me," I said, leaping up as my pulse began to race. "I just have to go and . . . do something."

"What?" my friend asked.

"Uh . . . I'll explain later."

We hurried off and quickly spotted Liz, who led me to Madonna, who was just moments away from going out onstage.

The show was just about to begin, and Madonna was wearing her black stage costume, with a pair of thigh-high leather boots for the opening number. She looked incredible, and she came over to me with her hand outstretched.

"I'm so happy to finally meet you," she said, grinning.

I took her hand, but I couldn't say a word. In my head, the word *finally* was spinning round and round. Surely the only way to understand it was that Madonna had been *looking forward* to meeting me?! I managed to blurt out something idiotic and meaningless, but the whole time I was thinking, *Not only does Madonna know I exist, she actually wanted to meet me!*

I knew how ridiculous my smile must be, but it was like I couldn't make my face do anything else. Madonna excused herself and headed off to do the show. Feeling completely overwhelmed, we went back to our seats to watch the show. The whole experience was so surreal that I needed a moment to really take it in and acknowledge that it had actually happened.

Before long, I was completely focused on the show. Madonna was just as amazing as I had expected, but there was one small detail that bothered me. Afterward, when I made a video reviewing the show, I said that I thought she'd played a little too much guitar.

I got a call from her manager the very next day, asking if I could stay in Vegas a while longer, attending her second and final show there before the tour moved on to Denver.

"Sure!" I said without even pausing to consider it.

The night before, we'd had great seats maybe ten rows back from the stage, but when I got to the MGM Grand Garden Arena for the second time, I realized I had been given the front row. *This is awesome!* I thought; I felt so happy.

But partway through the show, Madonna came out onto the stage with a guitar. She moved over to the mic, shading her eyes with one hand and looking straight at me, like she knew exactly where I was.

"My friend Perez is in the audience," she said. "But he thinks I play too much guitar in my show."

It felt like every single person in the audience was suddenly staring at me, and before I knew it, my face was bright red.

Still looking straight at me, Madonna said, "Deal with it, baby!"

With that, she played the first chord, and the audience cheered. I shuddered with joy, because it felt like I—*me!*—was part of Madonna's show. It got even better when she came on for an encore and played "Give It 2 Me," because she suddenly held out the mic for me to sing along.

I knew the words by heart, of course, and gave it my all. Honestly, it was beyond my wildest dreams.

———

Something similar happened again several years later, when I went to see Britney perform at Planet Hollywood. After she got me up onstage, she put a leash on me and began dragging me around like a dog while she sang "Freakshow." I had no problem with it—I actually thought it was pretty funny, and put my heart into running around on all fours. As it happened, it wasn't the first time a superstar had put a leash on me and made me her bitch.

In fact, Rihanna had already walked me like I was a dog several years earlier. It all started when someone from her team got in

> **After she got me up onstage, she put a leash on me and began dragging me around like a dog while she sang "Freakshow."**

touch in December 2010, asking if I wanted to be featured in the video for "S&M."

I was just about to say a spontaneous "Sure!" when I remembered having posted some leaked nudes of Rihanna a few years earlier. I really didn't want any drama, so I cleared my throat and cautiously asked, "Is Rihanna OK with this?"

"Yeah, it was her idea to have you," said the person on the other end of the line.

That immediately put all my worries to bed, so I said, "Oh, OK, then let's do it!"

I had already met Rihanna a bunch of times, and I had even reached out to her team to ask if she'd perform at my birthday party the previous March. To my surprise, she not only agreed to do it but she was willing to sing for free. Sadly, the whole Chris Brown thing happened around the Grammys (I still remember how shocked I was when I saw her bruised face), so she didn't come after all. Fortunately, I got lucky and managed to once more book Christina Aguilera to perform in her place.

In any case, I was nervous and excited that winter's day in January 2011 when I left my home in L.A. and got behind the wheel to drive out to the location for the shoot. I started the engine and cast an appreciative—or accepting, at least—glance at myself in the rearview mirror. I had moved on from the crazy colors of 2007 and had black hair. I'd also lost quite a lot of weight.

It was a long drive, but it turned out to be worth it, because when I arrived and met Rihanna for the first time in a while, I was struck by just how warm she was. I mean, she could not have been nicer to me, and made me feel at ease right away.

I was only supposed to be in one scene with her, and she would walk me around like her dog.

"How does that feel?" Melina Matsoukas (the director) asked me.

"Good, I guess," I told her with a shrug.

"We want you to wear these," a girl from the production team told me, holding up a pair of pink shorts.

"No problem!"

I changed into them and was given a pink PVC cap and a leash, and we filmed a scene where, among other things, I lifted one leg and pretended to pee on a pink lamppost with a happy look on my face.

Around the same time Chris Brown also asked me to appear in one of his videos, but I definitely said no to that!

24

The Big Fallout

*I manage to guide the conversation in the wrong direction
and wind up losing a friend.*

In 2011, I partnered with a production company to make a
series of specials that we sold around the world. Lady Gaga
was the first potential guest star who came to mind. The three
others I featured were Enrique Iglesias, Kelly Rowland, and Katy
Perry, but Gaga's episode was the one I was most looking forward to working on, since it would give us an opportunity to be
together.

She had just released the album *Born This Way* and was topping charts across the world again. By this point, she was no
longer simply a major artist—she was a global phenomenon. We
were still best friends—in my eyes, at least—so unlike everyone
else who wanted to interview her, I didn't have to send my questions to her publicist to scrutinize and approve in advance. Gaga
and I assumed, like the good friends we were, that neither of us
wanted to hurt the other.

In the United States, the show was called *Perez Hilton All Access*, and it was broadcast on the CW. In the UK, it had a different title, *Perez Hilton Superfan*, and it was shown on ITV2.

One cool part of the show was that we would do different activities with the guest stars. The producers and I decided that for the Lady Gaga episode, we would cook, and when I mentioned this to Gaga, she didn't have any objections. The whole thing just felt fun, and that didn't change when we started filming in L.A. Gaga was in a good mood, and we were joking together like we always did.

That's why, when the day came for me to get on a plane to Australia to do the last few interviews with Gaga—she was over there doing promo for the album—I wasn't the least bit worried about anything going wrong. In fact, I was looking forward to finishing off the funniest episode of the series.

I checked in to the InterContinental in Sydney, and as far as I remember, we started to record later that same day. Looking back, that seems like a dumb decision. Gaga was jet-lagged and tired when we went out to the house we were renting for the shoot, and I guess she hadn't eaten anything for hours.

In any case, the team began filming as Gaga and I cooked, with me asking her questions or just chatting with her about anything and everything. For some reason, we didn't eat any of the food we made, though we really should have. Instead, we drank wine, and before long Gaga moved on to spirits, knocking back the first glass before I even had time to blink.

Drinking while jet-lagged and hungry has unwanted consequences, of course, but that didn't seem to occur to any of us right there and then. It didn't become clear until a couple of hours later, once the catastrophe had already begun to unfurl.

From the kitchen, we took our glasses to an adjoining room, where Gaga changed her outfit before we sat down on a bed to continue the conversation—which, technically speaking, was an interview. The film crew set up the lighting and sound while Gaga and I drank and chatted. I still hadn't noticed anything off about her, aside from the fact that she occasionally seemed to get a slightly absent look in her eye. But I just chalked that up to the long flight.

Eventually, it was time for the next take, and I asked a few introductory questions to get the conversation going again. By this point, Gaga was already onto her third or fourth Jameson, and I noticed—with a certain amount of anxiety—that she was starting to get drunk. She was having trouble keeping her eyes focused on me.

I didn't know any better, so I didn't stop the interview and continued to ask the questions I had prepared on the plane. One of them was about her boyfriend, which I felt was relevant, but before I asked that particular question, I had another about her single "Judas," which had been a little controversial. I personally didn't find the track or the video the least bit controversial, but many others did. That was why I thought it was worth bringing up.

Gaga clearly didn't share that view, because her eyes turned dark and she snapped at me, "What are you doing? Are you trying to make me look bad?"

I hadn't expected that reaction at all, and I stared at her, completely at a loss as to what to say. All I managed was, "No, no, absolutely not. I just thought it was . . . uh . . . let's forget it. Sorry."

I looked down at my notes, desperate to move on to the next question and smooth over my mistake, which was still a huge mystery to me. I guess it was because of that confusion that the warning bells didn't start to ring. If I had just taken a moment to think things through, I would have realized it wasn't the right time to talk to Gaga about her love life, not when she was so clearly off balance.

But because I was also jet-lagged and, above all, stressed out by the whole situation, I looked up from my notes and said, "OK, so let's talk about your boyfriend instead."

For a split second, I thought Gaga was about to throw the glass at my face. But instead she leapt up from the bed and glared down at me before hissing, "What are you doing? I don't want to talk about this."

Yet again, I was completely taken by surprise, and I still had zero idea what I had done wrong, so I said, "I'm not asking anything bad, I just brought him up."

But by this point, Gaga seemed convinced I was trying to catch her out. If she hadn't been so drunk and if she had just thought it through, she would have seen that that was pretty much the last thing I wanted. But instead, she cracked her neck and said, "I'm ending this."

And with that, she staggered away.

It was like I was paralyzed for a few seconds, but then I jumped up and rushed to catch up with her.

"I'm not trying to make you look bad," I said, realizing that tears were streaming down my cheeks. "I'm your friend and your biggest champion."

But Gaga continued her unsteady journey out through the door. It made no difference how much I begged or cried, she refused to continue the interview, and headed back to her hotel.

I was in shock and didn't know what to say to the film crew once I got back to the house. They stared at me in bewilderment, as confused by what had just happened as I was. None of us had any idea what we should do next.

Eventually, I managed to compose myself somewhat and did what I could to get ahold of her. I sent her a text and eventually managed to get her on the phone—but only with her manager on the line as an intermediary. Gaga was as hostile to me as she had been earlier, no matter how many desperate apologies I made. It took several days of genuine regret, pleading, and tears before she finally agreed to finish the recording. It took place last minute, because we all had to fly back to the States the next day.

Though Gaga and I were talking again, something had changed between us. What was perfectly clear was that we had both lost our trust and respect. Our relationship was no longer the same, and that realization truly hurt me, because I cared deeply about her. It was a deep love.

Once I was back home and had managed to put a little distance between myself and the catastrophe, I realized there was a certain pattern to Gaga's behavior. What I saw wasn't pretty, but after mulling the thought over for a while, it dawned on me that Gaga was simply so big now that she no longer needed me the way she had at the beginning of her career. That day in Sydney must have been the moment when she first realized that herself.

Our big falling out meant that we stopped spending any time together. We stopped talking on the phone and had no contact whatsoever.

———

I wouldn't hear from her again until 2013—almost two years

later—when I found myself moving to New York again. There are a lot of things to consider when you're looking for a place to live: location, rent, the way the apartment is laid out, its proximity to shops and restaurants, etc.

On one of my first days there, I had no fewer than eight apartments to see in different parts of Manhattan. By the third or fourth, I was starting to get bored, but then I arrived at a block where I saw an apartment that, to my surprise, I immediately liked. I told the realtor, who couldn't hide how relieved he was.

It seemed like everything had fallen into place. Or it did until I sat down at my computer later that day, and got a huge shock. My inbox was overflowing with hate mail claiming that I was a pig who was tormenting Lady Gaga. After reading a few of the messages, I realized that Gaga had tweeted something about me earlier that day, so I checked what she had written. That was when I got another shock. She accused me of following her, of being a creepy stalker. My head was spinning. Had she gone completely crazy? Was she so drunk or high on drugs that she had finally lost all sense of reality?

But then, after reading another couple of tweets, I realized what had happened. Though I hadn't known it at the time, it turned out Gaga had an apartment in the same building I had visited just a few hours earlier. A fan of hers had spotted me there, and immediately tweeted the news to Gaga, who freaked out and started writing all those awful things about me on Twitter.

I had a short-term rental while I was going to viewings, and on that particular afternoon my yoga teacher was supposed to be coming over for a session. I just couldn't switch off, so instead of giving the usual yoga lesson, she gave me a massage as I cried loudly and uncontrollably.

I mean, it was a complete coincidence that I'd gone to a viewing in the same building where Gaga lived. Why, after two years' silence, would I suddenly start stalking her? It was sheer persecution mania, and once I got over the initial shock and deleted all the hate mail, I actually just felt sad for her.

She became incredibly famous very quickly, and sometimes that changes people for the worse. Fame can be very toxic. Fame can destroy people, and it can definitely destroy relationships.

Lady Gaga no longer hangs out with any of the people she was close to at the start of her career. Old friends, her entire team of songwriters, managers, producers, stylists—they've all been replaced.

Now, with the benefit of hindsight, I can see that Gaga was clearly hurting. She was hurting and that meant she hurt others. "Hurt people hurt people," as they say.

What upset me most was that before she became famous, I honestly thought she was my friend. But who knows, maybe we were never really friends. Maybe she was just using me the whole time, tossing me aside once she didn't need me anymore.

I guess I'll probably never know.

25

A Ton of Regrets

Ariana Grande gives me the cold shoulder, so I begin spending an
inexcusable amount of time writing mean things about her.

When celebrities are asked if they have any regrets, they
always say something like "No, everything I've done and
been through has made me
into the person I am today."
Not me. I have a ton of
regrets, particularly because
I now see that I never needed
to be so mean or cruel. I
would've been fine anyway,
just by being who I was.

**I have a ton of regrets,
particularly because I now
see that I never needed to
be so mean or cruel.**

One of the many things I regret—aside from drawing dicks
all over pictures of celebrities and things like that—is that I hurt
so many people by giving them nasty nicknames, and above all
that I was unkind to the children of celebrities. Some of them
were really young, others teenagers, and it makes no difference

that I really believed in what I was writing. I also regret that I thought it was OK to out celebrities. That is something I no longer believe.

There are also a number of career decisions that proved catastrophic, which I now regret. One example is the fact I turned down being the host of a reunion special of the reality show *Bad Girls Club* for the fourth year in a row. The premise of the show was that they put seven aggressive, disturbed girls in the same house for three months, and filmed them fighting with one another—often physically. This was around 2010, and the personal changes I was going through meant I felt uncomfortable with the raw, heartless tone of the show. That was the main reason I pulled out, but it was a decision I came to regret. After all, if you want to do TV, you have to be on TV.

Another thing that bothers me is the thought of all the millions I lost in legal fees, as well as the money I wasted during my breakthrough, while the site was expanding really quickly. As I mentioned earlier, I was working out of my apartment with my sister—then it was me, my sister, and one employee. Before long, I had a couple employees, and suddenly we had moved into this really fancy office building. That was the first mistake. I really didn't need a fancy office building in Beverly Hills.

Not only that, I really didn't need to spend so much money redecorating the office and building a studio there. The more money I made, the more I invested it back into the website. That's what you're told to do, but I regret following that advice. My biggest regret is that I didn't save more of the money I made. There were a few years when I was making millions of dollars, but I wasted most of it. The truth is that when you're making money, you stupidly think it will be like that forever.

My parents never taught me how to handle my money well. After all, Dad died when I was really young, and Mom frittered away all the money he left her in life insurance. She eventually ended up filing for bankruptcy, just like I did in my midtwenties.

For a few years, I was also living out a kind of fantasy of being a music manager. I pumped a lot of money into artists like Kalie Shorr, R&B sister act VanJess, plus a boy band called IM5, which I created in partnership with Jamie King and Simon Fuller—who was responsible for the Spice Girls and *American Idol*.

In 2011, Ariana Grande and her mother came over to my place to discuss the possibility of me managing her music career. I could see the potential in her, but they ultimately decided not to go with me—even as a consultant, an idea I had pitched to them. I was really hurt, so for years afterward I was super petty toward Ariana on my website and on social media. I regret that.

This book is the first time I've shared that story, and I'd like to apologize to Ariana and her mom. I'm really sorry. I should have apologized sooner, and for that I'm sorry too. Ariana has done pretty well for herself regardless. And like Lady Gaga and countless others, my ability to spot a star before they go global has always been exceptional.

Sadly, that didn't stop me from hiring another manager to help run my music business. I lost all the money I invested and didn't make a single cent, but I did have a lot of fun.

In truth, there are just two things I *don't* regret blowing a whole load of money on. The first is all the expensive vacations

I took with Mom and Barby, to places like China, India, Argentina, and Peru. Those were all magical.

The other is my kids.

2012

WHITNEY HOUSTON DIES.

DRAKE AND CHRIS BROWN GET INTO A FIGHT IN A NEW YORK NIGHTCLUB.

PRINCE HARRY IS PHOTOGRAPHED NAKED IN VEGAS.

A MASSEUR ACCUSES JOHN TRAVOLTA OF SEXUALLY HARASSING HIM AFTER REQUESTING A HAPPY ENDING DURING A MASSAGE. MORE MASSEURS SOON COME FORWARD WITH SIMILAR STORIES.

TOM CRUISE AND KATIE HOLMES GET DIVORCED.

FRED WILLARD IS ARRESTED FOR PUBLIC MASTURBATION.

26

I Become a Father

A woman I don't know gives birth to my son,
who begins his life by shitting on me.

For me it was never a question of *if* I have kids but *when*. Look-ing back now, I think I must have subconsciously decided early on to start a family on my own when the time came, partly because I didn't want to have to worry about the relationship possibly breaking down and only getting to see my children every other week. The thought of that kind of arrangement felt alien, unbearable.

I also knew that it would be a problem if my partner turned out to have completely different ideas about raising kids than I did. Because the truth is that I have a number of firm beliefs, most of them based on things that were good and bad during my own childhood. One example of this is that I wanted to seriously curb the amount of TV my children watched from an early age.

At the same time, there is a certain anxiety about single parenthood that I'm sure a lot of women also feel—about having sole responsibility and giving up your career for your child.

But by the time I was thirty-three, my longing for a child had grown so strong that it pushed everything else to one side. My professional success was also a positive, because I felt financially secure and able to provide a good life for my child.

By the time I was thirty-three, my longing for a child had grown so strong that it pushed everything else to one side.

So, in early 2012, I got in touch with a surrogacy agency that handled everything, from egg donors to the fertility clinic, surrogates to a lawyer. Back then, it was still quite unusual to start a family through surrogacy, and I had to go through an interview with an independently appointed court observer. They wanted to make sure I could be a good parent, that I was suitable to be granted full custody of my own biological child.

After that, it was time for the next stage: going through the catalogs of egg donors. I remember that the agency began by giving me a book of VIP donors, full of former beauty queens. But I explained that I had met enough women like that and asked to see a selection of more normal, less appearance-oriented women instead.

In the end, I settled on a cute but ordinary girl who was studying to become a nurse. That was the only thing I learned about her, and she didn't get to find out anything about me.

I was actually given a chance to get to know her over Skype, but it was my sister who ended up speaking to her. The conversation went well, and I remember turning to my mom and sister afterward and enthusiastically telling them, "She seemed really nice! I think I'm gonna pick her."

They both laughed.

"What?!" I asked. I couldn't see what was so funny.

"Nice isn't genetic," my sister told me, shaking her head.

But "nice" also wasn't the only reason I chose that particular woman. I also picked her for her looks. I chose a woman who looked like she could be my cousin, because that way, the kids would look a lot like me.

———————

During the spring of 2012, I also appeared as myself in two episodes of *Glee*. I didn't even have to audition for it; the show's creator, Ryan Murphy, reached out to me and asked if I would be interested. *Glee* was a huge pop culture sensation at the time, and I was a huge fan of the show, so I instantly said yes.

Pretty soon afterward, I found out that I would be acting alongside Lindsay Lohan, which I knew would bring even more attention to my part. We had a long history, and were a little like brother and sister: sometimes we got along, sometimes we didn't. It had been that way since the very beginning, when she started coming to see me at the Coffee Bean & Tea Leaf.

In any case, the first day of filming at Paramount Studios went relatively smoothly. Sure, Lindsay didn't really know her lines, but that was OK—she learned them quickly enough.

The second day proved more problematic, because Lindsay didn't show at all. At least not during the first four hours of the shoot, anyway.

I was supposed to be filming with both Lindsay and another actor named Rex Lee at a high school downtown, but because only Rex and I showed up, the crew had to reconfigure the entire filming schedule. On top of that, Lindsay was in a super crappy mood when she finally got there, and rather than apologize for her late arrival she refused to sit down with me and Rex to do what is known in the business as *coverage*—meaning the cameras film your back or other body parts while another actor is the focus of the shot.

Lindsay paced back and forth, irritated, and then turned to the shoot manager. "Why can't you get a fucking stand-in to do the coverage for me?"

I don't recall what the manager said, but I do remember that not long after, Lindsay went off for a cigarette break without letting anyone know, and that she kept doing that practically every five minutes for the rest of the day, which just made the whole shoot even slower.

All in all, it was a bit of a nightmare. Lindsay was a total diva. Despite that, I still have a soft spot for her, and we still talk on the phone sometimes.

———

While all this was going on, the surrogate I chose got pregnant on the first attempt, and though I'm pretty open about most things in my life, I decided to keep it quiet. The only people who knew were my mom, my sister, my lawyer, and my business manager. I knew far too much about how people work to give them a chance to get at me during this sensitive time. I was also afraid they would try to find out who the surrogate was and hound her to such an extent that she developed complications.

I guess I thought about these things more than I really want to admit—even to myself—because when I found out that she was pregnant, I was so emotional I could barely concentrate on my work. Everything suddenly felt so real, and I hurried to find someone who could transform one of the bedrooms into a nursery for me. Another part of the preparations involved picking and employing a suitable baby nurse.

My son wasn't due to arrive before March 2013, but as I was making my way to a Pink concert a month before the scheduled date, I got a call from the surrogate's husband telling me her water had broken.

I remember jumping into the back of a cab and racing home to pack a bag and catch the next plane to Oregon, where she was due to give birth. But the thought that I might not make it in time was so stressful I had to ask the driver to pull over so I could jump out and take a few deep breaths outside before taking another taxi home. I was frantic.

Things didn't get any better when I discovered it was too late to catch a flight that day. I called my business manager and asked whether I should charter a private plane, but he advised me to take the first plane the next morning instead.

I did as he said, but I didn't get a wink of sleep that night. My mother even had to give me a pill (the woman has everything). I was a complete mess the next morning, packing things without really knowing what I was doing.

Eventually, I managed to make it to the airport and onto the plane. But when I got to Portland, I was still so stressed that I went to the wrong hospital—there were two that had almost the exact same name. I jumped into another cab, and judging by the driver's reaction, I must have been acting like a complete madman. Not that I cared—the only thing that mattered was making it in time.

I finally made it to the right hospital, and it was as though my son had been waiting for me.

Thankfully, I did. I finally made it to the right hospital, and it was as though my son had been waiting for me.

Sweaty but relieved, I was there for the entire birth, and it was so intense that I was completely exhausted afterward, when a nurse came over with my son, who I later named Mario Armando Lavandeira III, after my father. She handed him to me, and I felt so happy I could burst. I also felt something else and turned over the hand that had been beneath his ass. It was covered in jet-black, sticky poop.

Ordinarily, I'm a very tidy person, and I get grossed out easily. But in that moment, I didn't care. The important thing was that my son was healthy, and just a few days later it was time to take him back to Los Angeles.

Over the weeks that followed, I dived head first into my new role as his father, trying to get into a routine that worked for us—like

feeding him every two and a half hours, just to make sure he put on weight.

Before long, I relaxed, and realized I didn't have to know *exactly* what he needed as soon as he started to cry. The important thing was that he was fed, bathed, and loved.

The name I gave him turned out to be a better fit than I could ever have imagined—my son is a wonderful physical reminder of my father. Sometimes when I look at him, I actually think he looks more like Dad than me.

I decided there was no real reason to keep him secret any longer and announced his birth on my website. In no time at all, the news was trending everywhere—something that confirmed I had made the right decision by choosing not to say anything sooner. Especially because a lot of the reactions were negative.

Not long after, I began to think about having a second child. Since I come from a big Latino family, surrounded by relatives and friends almost constantly, I had always pictured myself having several children.

There was no longer any doubt in my mind that it was the right decision, and I began the process of becoming a father for a second time. That's when I moved back to New York with Mom and my son, getting in trouble for looking at an apartment in the building Lady Gaga happened to live in. I wanted more balance in my life; I could be more social in New York, spending time with old friends before the next baby arrived.

But the second time around proved much trickier. The first attempt didn't work, and nor did the second or third. Since each round cost so much money, I grew nervous that it would never work.

I guess I had assumed it would be as easy and painless as the first time around, but I quickly learned that just because you want a child, that is no guarantee it will actually happen. Not even when you have the latest science on your side.

That made me humble, and particularly thankful for my son. Two years earlier, I had actually dedicated my children's book, *The Boy with Pink Hair* to him, with the words "Hope to see u soon."

2013

BEYONCÉ LIP-SYNCS THE AMERICAN NATIONAL ANTHEM AT PRESIDENT OBAMA'S INAUGURATION.

LEAH REMINI LEAVES SCIENTOLOGY.

SIMON COWELL GETS HIS FRIEND'S WIFE PREGNANT

MILEY CYRUS TWERKS IN A BIKINI AT THE MTV VIDEO MUSIC AWARDS.

OWEN WILSON'S MARRIED PERSONAL TRAINER IS PREGNANT WITH HIS BABY.

27

Dating as Perez Hilton

I buy myself a super expensive pied-à-terre in
New York City for my second big whore phase.

Dating has always been extra challenging for me. The truth is that it's impossible to date as Perez Hilton. Most gay men dislike me or even hate me. Some look down on what I do, and others are Lady Gaga fans who hate me because they want to be loyal to her. To put it simply: even if I meet someone who doesn't dislike me for what I do or what I've done, it can still be a problem if their friends hate me.

Some time ago, I posted a photo of this hot young dude on my Instagram account and tagged him. He reposted me, saying, "Get the fuck out of my Instagram! I don't like you."

If I were hot, or physically attractive, I would be able to get away with so much more in the gay community, but I'm not. I'm a normal-looking dude, and I have to try to make the most of that. I'm not saying that because I'm bitter, it's just the truth. If I was on a successful TV show, I'm sure it would be much easier, too. Then guys would start messaging me on Instagram. I wouldn't mind being used; I would use them back.

Still, if I had to choose, I'd rather have a successful TV show than a boyfriend. After all, boyfriends come and go, and sad as it

If I had to choose, I'd rather have a successful TV show than a boyfriend.

is to say, a successful TV show would help me find a boyfriend. That might sound cynical, but I truly believe that there is someone out there for me. That person will be strong, and he'll be willing to get to know the real me.

Some gay men don't like me because they think I'm too flamboyant, but the truth is that I'm an introverted extrovert. I guess I've built up a guard to protect myself, and that might be one of the reasons why several years have passed since I last had sex. Don't get me wrong, I'm not sad about that, because I masturbate regularly. Almost daily, to be honest, and I thoroughly enjoy that. I enjoy that it's quick. I don't have to spend a lot of time looking for sex. I don't even need to try to look for sex.

But when I moved back to NYC in 2013, things were different. It started like a second slut phase for me. When I lived in New York for the first time in my early twenties, I was a big whore. But when I became Perez and gained a ton of weight, for the longest time I didn't have sex.

New York City is the most magical place on earth. It's easy to find people who share your passions and interests, but there are also so many more gay men there, so many more options.

The minute I moved back, I signed up for the dating site OkCupid. It was great, but I quickly discovered a problem: since

I now had a kid, I could no longer—or, to be accurate, no longer wanted to—take anyone home. That was why I got myself a studio apartment in the same building where I was already living. The rent on that fuck pad cost me almost $4,000 a month, and I also paid an interior design firm to redecorate it, which was insanely expensive. But I was making more money then, so I felt comfortable spending what would feel like a fortune today.

In any case, that studio apartment meant I could ask guys, "Can we meet at my place?" It was super convenient, and I would set up multiple dates every week—often more than one a night. I treated dating like Vegas, going for volume and hoping to hit the jackpot.

I used to suggest meeting up for coffee first. That's a great approach, because you can tell in the first three or four minutes if there's any chemistry and if it's going to work out. If I knew it wasn't going to work out, I didn't have to waste any more time than necessary and had only a short walk home.

I didn't really meet anyone great, but I came close once. The guy ended things at the *start* of our seventh date. Looking back, I've often wondered why he didn't wait until after dinner, or once we had seen the show we had tickets to. Or why he didn't just cancel the whole thing so we could have escaped suffering through that evening together.

I had really fallen for this guy, and I thought he felt the same way, so I was completely floored when he said, "I think we should just be friends."

I wanted to ask why, of course, whether something had happened to make him feel differently, but before I had time to ask, he continued, "We should probably get going to the restaurant if we want to make the show in time." He looked down at his watch.

I stared at him, trying to work out whether he was kidding, but clearly he intended to stick to our plans, despite having just ended the relationship.

I followed him to the restaurant and from there to the theater. I had bought us tickets to a Joan Rivers show, and though I loved Joan I had real trouble focusing as I sat beside my completely indifferent ex—or whatever he was.

It was *the* most awkward date I've ever been on, and after that evening, I never saw him again.

————————

Now that I'm living in Los Angeles again, my dating life has ground to a halt. The move across the country was a real culture shock, because I discovered that the dating site I got plenty of interest on in New York, OkCupid, got very little attention in L.A.

Sure, I went on a few dates, but after a couple years, I lost interest in the site somehow. I wasn't interested in trying to find a partner in one of the bars in West Hollywood, either, purely because I would never dare go up to someone unless that person was openly flirting with me.

These days, I just keep hoping I'll meet someone through work or at the gym or my kids' school. If I'm honest, one of the reasons I had kids was to prepare for the possibility that I might never have a husband or boyfriend. That's a fact, and a possibility for anybody, but maybe more so for me.

Sometimes I wonder if I'm single because I've always had my parents as role models, and they had such a great marriage. They never argued and they never cheated on each other. What they had was more than love—it was mutual worship.

I always had a premonition that I would never be in a long-term relationship until I was in my fifties, purely because a lot of gay men aren't ready to settle down before they hit that age.

I'll be in my early fifties when my kids start leaving home to go to college, so if I don't have a boyfriend by then I'll make it my full-time mission to find one. Hopefully people's perceptions of me will have changed by then. Who knows, they might not even remember the awful things I did.

2014

THE BILL COSBY RAPE ALLEGATIONS COME TO LIGHT.

RAY RICE PHYSICALLY ABUSES HIS FIANCÉE JANAY PALMER, PUNCHING HER SO HARD SHE IS KNOCKED TO THE GROUND.

ACTOR STEPHEN COLLINS CONFESSES TO CHILD MOLESTATION.

BETTE MIDLER CALLS ARIANA GRANDE A WHORE.

BASED ON A RECOLLECTION IN HER MEMOIR, LENA DUNHAM IS ACCUSED OF MOLESTING HER SISTER WHEN THEY WERE BOTH CHILDREN.

28

———

Howard Stern

I create radio history with my finger.

I had been living in New York with my mom and young son for almost a year when, in the summer of 2014, I was invited to take part in Howard Stern's show on SiriusXM radio.

Howard is a living legend, and he has a solid reputation for being completely unpredictable and boundless—in a very entertaining way. Since I had been on his show before, I knew what to expect: absolutely anything. But it felt OK, because I liked Howard and thought of it as an honor to be his guest. The studio was just seven blocks from my apartment, so it didn't take long to get there that morning.

During the first five minutes of the interview, nothing much happened—nothing that shocked me, anyway, or knocked me off center. Then, out of nowhere, someone on the show brought up a bet that Howard had made with Benjy, a chubby white guy in a cap sitting on a couch at the other end of the studio.

I knew that Benjy was actually Benjy Bronk, part of Howard's team, so I waved to him and smiled, but Benjy didn't return the gesture. Instead, his eyes wandered nervously, which piqued my curiosity.

"Benjy said that if he couldn't lose twenty pounds in a month," Howard continued, grinning at Benjy, "he had to let someone finger him."

Out of nowhere, I was asked if I could finger Benjy.

I took a deep breath. It felt like my life was flashing before my eyes. Was he serious? I stared at Howard, who continued to look at me with that devilish grin on his lips. It was clear: he wasn't joking; this was some of that stupid shit that straight dudes are always doing.

The situation was completely surreal, and I thought in panic, *What am I gonna do, what am I gonna say?* I knew that if you agreed to do *The Howard Stern Show*, you knew what you were signing up for, and I felt like I had no choice but to join in, so I said yes. Still, I immediately asked a counterquestion of my own: "Why me?"

"We thought you'd be a good fit for the job," Howard told me, as though it were the most obvious thing in the world. Clearly they had taken it for granted I would say yes.

"But," Howard continued, a concerned frown appearing on his brow, "we do have a bit of a problem."

"OK . . . ?" I said hesitantly, wondering what was coming next.

"Yeah," said Howard. "The thing is, we can't do any penetration in this building. It's against the law."

If I had wanted to get myself out of the situation, I could have just said, *That's a shame*, and quickly changed the topic or found some reason to leave the studio early. But clearly I didn't want to be saved, because I heard myself say, "We could do it at my place. It's not far from here."

Howard's face lit up, and he said, "Great, then let's do that!"

It didn't take long for the guys to gather all the equipment they needed, and we were soon ready to head over there. Everyone but Benjy was noticeably excited, and I remember thinking that this could be something out of the ordinary.

Everyone but Benjy was noticeably excited, and I remember thinking that this could be something out of the ordinary.

It was almost nine thirty in the morning when Howard suddenly said, "Let's go!"

On command, everyone marched out of the studio, and I followed them out. We took the elevator down to the lobby and began walking to the building where I had three apartments: one for me and my son, one for Mom, and one that, as I already mentioned, I called my fuck pad.

After I unlocked the front door of the fuck pad, I took them straight into the bedroom, which felt like the right place for what they had planned.

It didn't take the team long to set up, so I quickly grabbed a tube of lube and pulled on the pair of plastic gloves they handed me. I saw Benjy's face turn white as he watched me pull on one of the gloves and squeeze out some lube onto my fingers. I smiled in a failed attempt to reassure him.

Benjy was sweating profusely, and it didn't help when Howard said, "OK, Benjy, drop your pants and get onto your knees on the bed. We're live in one minute."

I actually felt a little bad for him as he struggled out of his jeans and underwear and crawled up onto the bed. But I also felt kind of excited about the stunt, and as soon as we were broadcasting again, I didn't hesitate: I loosened Benjy's asshole with a few circular movements of my finger before pushing it all the way in.

"*Iiiih! Aaaah! Ooooh!*"

Benjy was making all kinds of weird sounds as he squirmed to get away from my finger. I thought he was overreacting, because it wasn't like I had shoved my entire hand up there.

"It's just *one* finger," I said to Howard with a knowing shrug. "Should I put another one in?"

Howard seemed tempted by my offer, but said, "No, I don't think Benjy would be able to handle the extra appendage."

So I had to make do with one finger, which I waggled a little to get more funny sounds out of him. The team were all laughing, with no compassion at all for my little sex slave. Eventually Howard decided Benjy had suffered enough, and he gestured for me to stop. I pulled out my finger with a popping sound, and Benjy quickly yanked his underwear and pants back up, avoiding all of our eyes.

For a moment, I felt guilty, and I thought, *Hope I haven't just scarred him for life!* But then I decided that the entire thing was so funny that I had to stop myself from laughing as I took off the glove.

For the rest of the day, I felt high from the experience, and at my gym that afternoon, one straight guy after another kept coming over to talk about what happened on Howard's show.

The truth is that far more heterosexual guys than gay guys like me and what I do. I think that's largely down to Howard Stern—his audience consists primarily of dudes, and I've been something of a recurring guest on his show.

The guys coming over to me wanted to know whether I had *really* fingered Benjy or whether it was all fake. I suddenly realized that to many of the listeners, it had sounded completely crazy and unbelievable. All I could do was confirm that it was all real. The guys thought that was so funny they completely broke down.

2015

MARVIN GAYE'S FAMILY WINS LAWSUIT AGAINST ROBIN THICKE AND PHARRELL OVER ACCUSATIONS THAT THEIR SONG "BLURRED LINES" WAS PLAGIARIZED FROM GAYE'S "GOT TO GIVE IT UP."

CHARLIE SHEEN REVEALS HE HAS HIV. BURT REYNOLDS SAYS HE DESERVES IT.

KYLIE JENNER POSES IN A WHEELCHAIR AS PART OF AN S&M PHOTO SHOOT FOR *INTERVIEW* MAGAZINE.

SCOTT WEILAND OF STONE TEMPLE PILOTS AND VELVET REVOLVER DIES AT FORTY-EIGHT.

JENNIFER GARNER AND BEN AFFLECK ANNOUNCE THEIR BREAKUP ONE DAY AFTER THEIR TENTH WEDDING ANNIVERSARY.

29

Celebrity Big Brother UK

I decide to start saying yes to things, and find myself in a torture chamber as a result.

Just a few months after I appeared on Howard Stern's radio show, legendary comic Joan Rivers died. We'd worked together a few times, and I had been a guest on two of her shows—one of which was a reality show she made with her daughter.

In any case, her death made me think about all kinds of things, including the fact that up to that point, I had been turning down opportunities left, right, and center. I would say stupid things like "That's lame" or "That's not a good fit with my brand," and I was too laser-focused on trying to get my own TV show. Now I just wanted any kind of show.

As I thought about Joan and her life, I realized I had to start saying yes to more things. That was what Joan always did, after all, and that was how she managed to enjoy a long, successful career.

One of the many offers I regretted turning down was *Celebrity Big Brother UK*, so I swallowed my pride and dug out the number of the woman who had contacted me about it. When she picked up, I hurried to explain that I had decided I'd like to take part in the show after all, so if they were still interested and ever had space for me . . .

I didn't get any further than that, because she practically shouted down the line, "Of course! I'm sure we can arrange for you to take part in the next season. I just need to check with my boss."

She called me back not long after and said they had penciled me in for the next season, which was due to start in January 2015.

"That's great," I said, before hesitantly asking how much they would pay. They gave me a figure that exceeded all expectations, though I was careful not to let her know that. Still, as happy as I was about the paycheck, I had no idea just how huge a mistake I was making by agreeing to take part without watching the show first.

The problem was that since I became an adult, I hadn't had time to watch TV. Even if I had, the idea of doing it on my own always seemed so sad to me. I never read the newspaper or listened to the radio, either. Sure, I consumed a ton of media on my laptop and cell phone, but that was all work.

To put it simply, I had no idea what I was saying yes to. All I knew about the show was what I had read on Wikipedia, and

my spontaneous reaction had been "That seems easy!" I didn't even bother to watch any of the episodes the production company sent over to me, and before I knew it I was getting on a plane to London.

That was why it came as such a shock to me on the first day of shooting when I realized that the other contestants and I would be locked in our bedroom overnight.

"They're kidding, right?" I said to one of the other housemates.

But it was true: the crew needed to be able to work on the set while we slept; that's when they prepared the following day's activities and challenges.

The next unpleasant surprise came that same evening, when they lowered a huge metal shutter that prevented us from seeing what they were doing outside the bedroom. It also prevented any daylight from coming in.

The feeling of being locked up hit me like a punch to the gut, and I had to force myself to stay calm. That would continue every night throughout the shoot.

———————

If it had been a mistake not to do my research before heading into the house, it was an even bigger issue that I hadn't immediately told the others that I was only there because I had decided to say yes to everything—for the money.

I didn't really want to be away from my young son, so drawing it out by trying to actually *win* the competition didn't interest me at all. Especially because I would make the same amount of money whether I was voted out first or if I stayed two weeks longer. I just wanted to go home as soon as possible, and was happy with the figure I had already been promised.

But I didn't say any of that until a week into the show, and everyone thought I was lying—that it was a tactic on my part, an attempt to fly under the radar and win the competition.

I had finally realized just how bad a situation I had gotten myself into.

"No, I swear, it's true!" I said, but the others just laughed and smiled mockingly.

By that point, I had finally realized just how bad a situation I had gotten myself into. It wasn't just the house—with its metal shutters, terrible air, bright lights, and cameras everywhere—that was driving me crazy, it was the people I was locked up with.

The worst of them was a woman named Katie Hopkins, who is a kind of British version of the political commentator Ann Coulter. I guess you could describe her as an ultra hardcore right-wing troll. She hates fat people, unemployed people, anyone with tattoos, people who weren't white or who had a different faith, as well as anyone whose sexual orientation differed from hers.

I guess that's why she hated me so much, and why she tried her best to make the others hate me too. The way she schemed to isolate me was nothing short of sadistic, and she was constantly trying to pick fights with me in an attempt to knock me off balance. I began to have anxiety attacks, and it didn't help that I was barely sleeping.

On top of the nightly drinking sessions my housemates insisted on having, which went on until the early hours every day, I had to share a bed with a guy who was both racist and homophobic—and if I turned the other way, I ended up right underneath an air vent, which blew cold air straight into my mouth. It was torture. I spent my nights shivering after having sweated all day under the spotlights.

But the biggest problem was probably that my mind was spinning as a result of all the people screaming at one another, and sometimes being genuinely threatening—like the guy who was suffering crack withdrawal and called me "faggot" with a murderous look in his eye.

After two weeks of getting two hours' sleep, at most, every

night, I was desperate, and couldn't bear the prospect of spending another two weeks in the studio. That was how long the competition would last, and simply dropping out wasn't an option, because that way I would only be paid a fifth of the amount we had agreed on.

My only real chance of getting out of there was to be voted out. You also could be kicked out as a result of serious personal issues or unacceptable behavior—something that happened to a guy who squeezed one of the other contestants' breasts. I decided to bank on the former.

Every time I threatened to drop out, they sent me to see the psychologist who was supposed to be there for the contestants, but I got no sympathy whatsoever. He didn't even take me seriously when I said that I was afraid of one of the other contestants.

"Listen to me," I said, trying to ignore his mocking smile. "The guy is coming down off hard drugs, I can tell. He's got withdrawal symptoms."

But the psychologist simply shook his head.

"You don't understand what I'm saying!" I practically screamed. "He's a dangerous crackhead, he could stab me with a kitchen knife any minute!"

This time, the psychologist rolled his eyes and said, "You're great entertainment. You're in the right place for that—you've probably got a good shot of getting to the final."

"But I don't want to be in the final! I want to leave before I go crazy!"

A few days later, I was in such bad shape that I went to see the doctor who came to the studio every day. And unlike the psychologist, he could see that I was on the verge of a breakdown, and he gave me some sleeping pills.

That night, I enjoyed a deep, dreamless sleep and didn't wake up until late the next morning. I later realized that all the others had been popping pills from day one, and that I could've saved myself all that unnecessary suffering by doing what they had.

After that, my remaining time in the studio became more bearable. Aside from Nadia Sawalha and Katie Price, none of the other housemates liked me, and when Nadia was voted out I was devastated. We weren't allowed any pens or paper in the house, but one of the sponsors was a makeup company, so I used nail polish to paint on tinfoil, on cans of beans, whatever I could find to keep myself entertained. Since we weren't allowed any reading material, either, I sometimes used to go to the pantry just to read the labels.

Despite the sleeping pills and attempts to keep myself busy, after just three weeks in the *Big Brother* house I felt like I had regressed back to childhood. It honestly felt like my brain had shrunk while I was in there, and during the fourth and final week, the production team brought in a social media expert who told us sensitive information about one another in an attempt to create conflict. That was when I finally got voted out.

By that point, I felt indifferent to the whole thing, despite the fact that the producers gushed over my performance, telling me it was the highest-rated series to date. They said I was the most talked-about person in the history of the show.

2016–2017

AMBER HEARD FILES FOR DIVORCE FROM JOHNNY DEPP.

GLEE'S MARK SALLING IS CHARGED WITH POSSESSION OF CHILD PORNOGRAPHY.

MOVIE PRODUCER HARVEY WEINSTEIN IS ACCUSED OF SEXUAL HARASSMENT OR ASSAULT BY MORE THAN FIFTY WOMEN.

50 CENT ALLEGEDLY TRIES TO PUNCH A FAN AT A CONCERT.

EMPIRE STAR MOROCCO OMARI IS ARRESTED AND CHARGED WITH DOMESTIC ABUSE.

MISCHA BARTON CLAIMS HER EX SECRETLY RECORDED THEM HAVING SEX.

NETFLIX FIRES KEVIN SPACEY FROM *HOUSE OF CARDS*.

30

A Home for Me and My Family ... and a Year of Pain

Illness and death make me take refuge in my alter ego.

Once I had recovered from my experience on *Big Brother* (which took a while), I bought a multifamily apartment building in Manhattan, just west of Eighth Avenue, in Chelsea. I paid a serious amount of money for it, but it was a five-unit building, and my thinking was that I could use three of the units for my own family—by this point in time, my daughter, Mia Alma, had been born—renting out the remaining two apartments and thus helping to pay off the mortgage.

The only problem was that I realized I hated everything about it almost as soon as I moved in. Mom did, too; the place just didn't feel like home.

Around the same time the deal went through, however, I was offered a part in an off-Broadway musical, a parody of the famous sitcom *Full House*. I said yes, and with that forgot all thoughts about where I was living.

We rehearsed for a few weeks and then the production company moved me and my family to Toronto, where we stayed in a house with plenty of space and a backyard. That was when I realized we needed to move back to L.A. It was now 2016, and I'd had three or four great years in New York City, but given how expensive it is to live there—plus the fact I was living beyond my means—I would have gone bankrupt again if I had stayed there.

I began house hunting in Los Angeles and immediately knew which area I wanted to live in. I also knew I wanted a pool and a guesthouse. There weren't many houses like that for sale, so I was ecstatic when one suddenly came on the market: it was almost a hundred years old, and it seemed to tick most of my boxes.

A few days later, I flew out for a viewing, and I knew from the minute I set foot inside that it was the one. It was actually the only house I saw.

Mom and her boyfriend of a decade moved into the guesthouse, and while she might be the biggest inspiration for how I *don't* want to live my life, there is also so much about her that I want to pass on to my own kids.

She's the reason my children's first language is Spanish, for example. In fact, we only speak Spanish at home, and I know that my son even *thinks* in Spanish, despite being perfectly fluent in English.

On October 4, 2017, my youngest daughter, Mayte Amor, also came into this world.

———————

Like anyone who has been on this earth for a while, I know all too well that happiness can quickly turn to despair. But it still came as a shock when Mom's boyfriend was suddenly taken ill. It turned out to be stage IV liver and gall bladder cancer.

He and Mom had been together for so long by that point that he was like a real member of the family. It suddenly felt like I was fourteen, losing my dad all over again. I thought I had left that grief behind, but I found myself battling with all kinds of emotions I didn't know how to handle.

On top of that, I had to be strong for Mom and the kids. They were still so young, but my son was old enough to know that *something* was wrong, and he looked up at me one day and asked, "Daddy, why do you and Grandma talk so quietly like that?"

I didn't know what to say and simply gave him an awkward pat on the head. I felt powerless to protect him from the pain I myself had experienced as a boy.

As Mom's boyfriend grew sicker and sicker, I had to tell him the truth. Though it was difficult, it was nothing compared to watching as the loss of yet another life partner slowly broke Mom down. This time, the process was much more drawn out than it had been when Dad died.

He fought the cancer for fourteen months, but in January 2019 it finally defeated him.

Sadly, Mom's boyfriend was barely in the ground before she discovered what looked like a zit on her vulva. Back in New York, she had been treated for skin cancer on one ear, and when she went to the doctor, she learned that it was back—albeit in an unexpected location.

"Is that even possible?" I asked in shock when she told me

what the doctor had said. To me, it sounded like something the devil would make up. It was *so* cruel, particularly considering what Mom had just been through.

They caught the cancer early, thankfully, at a stage when the doctors could still operate, but there were still complications. They didn't manage to remove all of the cancer the first time around, meaning she had to undergo surgery for a second time— just a few days before we were due to fly to Miami for spring break. Luckily the operation only took an hour or so, and she left the hospital the very same day.

"Are you sure you feel like traveling right now?" I asked her, but she gave me one of her typical answers: "Don't be stupid, of course I do."

But when we got home from Miami and she went for a checkup at the hospital, even she came close to losing her faith. The doctor told her she would have to have another operation. That was devastating news. Since Mom is diabetic, it takes an extra long time for her to recover from that type of procedure.

"Oh God," I said, utterly failing to stay strong for her. "But that means they'll have to give you anesthesia!" I panicked, because she'd had trouble with that in the past. I pictured one catastrophe after another.

By the day of the operation, I was practically a nervous wreck. Making matters even worse, when we met the doctor at the hospital, we learned that Mom's bladder had collapsed and that they would actually have to perform two operations at once.

The wait was awful, sitting on the fake leather couches in the sterile waiting room at Cedars-Sinai. The more time that passed, the more nervous and impatient I felt. Before long, I realized that the hospital staff were getting sick of my constant questions.

"How is it going?"

"Isn't the operation over yet?"

"Have there been any complications?"

"How did she react to the anesthetic?"

As I paced back and forth or sat on one of the couches, unable to think about more than one thing at a time, I realized just how close Mom and I were. She had become my best friend over the years, the person who understood me best. Losing her was one of the worst things I could imagine.

Eventually, after three nightmarishly long hours, one of the doctors finally emerged. "The operation—or *operations*—went to plan. She's doing well."

I breathed a huge sigh of relief and said, "Oh, thank you, God."

Because of Mom's diabetes, her recovery was long and difficult, and she fell into a depression that meant she didn't feel like leaving the house. Since we were living so close, sharing so much of our days, her moods also had an effect on me. What with her boyfriend's long, drawn-out illness and her own battle with cancer, I was completely exhausted.

I suppose that might be why I took refuge in my alter ego—Perez—and dyed my beard one crazy color after another. I guess you could say I needed him more than ever. Just like in 2007 and 2008, when I had all those crazy hair colors, I was in pain, and I tried to deal with that by putting on a mask, by putting on armor.

I also tried to escape by going on vacation—not once, but six times in as many months. As a result of that, another of my old habits also remerged: comfort eating.

I was in pain, and I tried to deal with that by putting on a mask, by putting on armor.

2018–2020

ROSEANNE IS CANCELED AFTER ROSEANNE BARR POSTS A RACIST TWEET.

JUSSIE SMOLLETT ALLEGEDLY FAKES A HATE CRIME.

MILEY CYRUS AND LIAM HEMSWORTH SPLIT.

ASAP ROCKY GOES TO JAIL IN SWEDEN.

PAMELA ANDERSON AND PRODUCER JON PETERS BREAK UP ONLY TWELVE DAYS AFTER THEY GOT MARRIED IN MALIBU, CALIFORNIA.

31

The Hills

*I finally get to appear in an episode of a show I've been
covering for years, but it's nothing like I imagined.*

In the first half of the 2000s, the MTV reality series *The Hills*
was a huge cultural phenomenon, and its stars were plastered
on the front of celebrity gossip magazines practically every week.
Online, no one was covering them like I was—nor as frequently.
The popularity of the show meant I was giving them about as
much attention as Britney, and one of the biggest stories I ever
broke was about *The Hills*—specifically, about the sex tape star
Lauren Conrad had made. This was in 2007, and while I'll never
reveal my sources, what I will say is that *The Hills* had a huge
cast, and more than one member told me that the tape existed.
So I wrote about it.

Lauren Conrad quickly came out to deny the existence of the
tape, and sure enough, it never materialized. Looking back now,
all I can assume is that my sources were lying to me. These people

had an agenda. But at the time, I had no reason to suspect they were lying. If I did, I never would have published the story.

In any case, I was desperate to be on *The Hills* myself, but I was never asked (even if I did turn up in an episode about one of the stars' weddings).

In 2018, however, when the production company decided to bring the show back as *The Hills: New Beginnings*, I got a call asking if I wanted to do an audition, essentially a Skype interview with a casting director. The interview I did was then cut down to a three- to four-minute presentation that they showed the network. In the end, they decided not to hire me, and picked Mischa Barton from *The OC* instead. They also cast Brandon Thomas Lee, son of Pamela Anderson and Tommy Lee.

Then one day, without warning, the producers got in touch because one of the stars, Spencer Pratt, had thrown a party I attended. But before I get into that, I need to tell you a little about Spencer, because the new-and-improved version is very different from the old Spencer.

I was friends, or on friendly terms, with all the stars of the original show, but old Spencer and I were definitely closest, and later had the biggest falling out. During the last few seasons of the original series, he became incredibly deluded and angry, even violent toward one of the producers. In the end, he was no longer even welcome to the wrap party, and as far as I'm concerned, he began writing awful tweets about my sister of all people—and I hardly need to point out that she hadn't done anything to him.

In any case, once *The Hills* ended, he and Heidi Montag (who also starred in the show) left L.A., and I didn't hear from him for a few years. That changed suddenly one day, when he invited me to take part in a new digital show he was doing for MTV, *Spencer Pratt Will Heal You.*

I don't really believe in crystals—I guess you could say I'm agnostic where they're concerned—but it turned out Spencer was *all about* crystals and had even started a business selling them. That was also why he had invited me to his party, in an attempt to advertise his business. Several of the others from *The Hills* were invited, along with the producers and various members of the film crew.

I went along primarily to see Spencer. When I arrived, he and Mischa Barton were chatting, but she ran off the minute she saw me. A producer of *The Hills* saw this and contacted me a few days later, asking if I'd like to appear in an episode of the revival show.

Looking back now, I can see that they needed me for Mischa's storyline. She must have earned a ton of money from the revival, but I guess the producers didn't get all that much from her— something I could've predicted in advance. Mischa isn't really a reality star; she's an actress, and I think she wants to keep acting, so she needs to be careful with how she behaves and how she comes across.

"OK," I said to the producer. "What do you want me to do?"

The producer cleared her throat and said, "I want you to come in and talk to Mischa about the past."

In truth, Mischa was one of the people I had been really awful to. I own that. I accept it, and therefore I knew there was a 95 percent chance I'd come across in a negative light. Still, I said yes, and at first everything seemed to be going well. I had made up my mind to hear her out; that seemed like the right thing to do. Once she was done speaking, I responded, sharing my truth. We got to a point, after filming for maybe fifteen minutes, where I thought the conversation was coming to an end, so I said, "Truly, no bullshit . . . I'm being totally serious now . . . I just want to tell you that I'm truly sorry for the things I did in the past. For the nasty nicknames I gave you. All the stories I wrote."

Mischa just stared at me, and eventually said, "I don't believe you."

"Well, I'm very serious. I swear on my kids' life."

But Mischa still didn't believe me, which I thought—and still do—was really odd. I mean, there's a difference between accepting my apology and not believing me when I swear on my kids' life!

32

I'm a Celebrity . . .
Get Me Out of Here!

I get buried alive with hundreds of snakes and have to
bungee jump twice against my will.

In November 2019, it felt like everything finally started to turn around, and it all began with an offer to take part in the Australian version of *I'm a Celebrity . . . Get Me Out of Here!*

I was really happy about it, because if there was one thing I wanted it was to appear on TV more. The fact that this new offer involved surviving in the jungle didn't faze me at all. Despite my experiences with *Celebrity Big Brother*, I'd done well on competitive reality TV before; a few years earlier, I was on a show called *Worst Cooks in America*—which I actually managed to win. In fact, I thought of it as a challenge, and decided to go into the show prepared—not making the same mistakes I had on *Big Brother*.

This time, I even got the opportunity to watch some of the show in peace and quiet before I joined, because the plan was for me to arrive as an "intruder" two weeks into the season. From the day I signed the contract, I began strength training twice a day, watching my diet, and avoiding coffee—because I knew that coffee was one of the many things I wouldn't have access to during the shoot.

In other words, I was in great shape when, in January 2020, I arrived in Kruger National Park in South Africa.

That turned out to be a huge mistake, because from my very first day there I realized just how little food we would be given. It was clearly a deliberate decision on the part of the production company, creating tensions in the group and making us work extra hard in their crazy challenges—the prize was always food. During the eight days I was on the show, I lost over ten pounds, and since I didn't have an ounce of fat to spare when I arrived in South Africa, I looked genuinely malnourished. In the end, I was allowed to speak to a psychologist, because I felt like the hunger was driving me crazy.

One good thing about my preparations meant that I was, at the very least, ready for all the challenges that were awaiting me, and even managed to be "buried alive" in a box with hundreds of snakes. As they slithered over me, I had to answer a whole bunch of questions about celebrities.

My heart was obviously racing, and I alternated between sweating and shivering. The more I freaked out, the more freaked out the snakes seemed to get, and they started wrapping around my arms, legs, and throat. Eventually, I worked out that I had to stay calm, so that's what I did. Or maybe I just resigned myself to it and managed to stay in the coffin for thirty minutes, getting all my answers right. Either way, I won the challenge.

Something similar happened when they asked me to do a bungee jump. I'd never done anything like that before, and looking back now, I can honestly say I'll never do it again.

You can do it, it's not dangerous . . . it's just really high, I told myself as I stood at the edge, holding a stupid giant pickle that I was supposed to drop in the middle of an enormous burger bun on the ground. I was terrified and closed my eyes as I jumped, meaning I missed the target completely. I also made the mistake of *jumping* rather than just allowing myself to fall.

When the hosts—who could clearly see how disappointed and angry I was with myself—gave me another chance, I listened to their advice. Second time around, I actually managed to hit the target!

The reason it went so well must've been because I was so hungry I was willing to do anything for food. I guess that's also why I managed another challenge involving eating a pizza with pig nipples on it, and one where I had to drink something called "the Colon"—a drink made of some animal's colon. It tasted like blood, and there were chunks of the animal's colon floating in it, plus some bugs on top for garnish.

It tasted like blood, and there were chunks of the animal's colon floating in it, plus some bugs on top for garnish.

Maybe it's not so surprising that when I left the competition after just over a week, I mostly felt relieved to leave the jungle. But before I could fly home, I had to give a whole bunch of interviews and be examined by the show's doctors and psychologist; I had to meet the publicist and God knows what else. When I finally set off for the tiny airport on the edge of the jungle, I hadn't slept for more than maybe ninety minutes in two days.

I was completely exhausted and could hardly keep my eyes open when I arrived at the Hoedspruit Airport building and went through the rudimentary security checks, boarding the plane. Landing in Johannesburg to change planes, I felt like I wanted to use the layover to get a little work done. So, I opened my bag to take out my laptop, and realized it wasn't there.

I felt a sudden chill, and began struggling to breathe.

Oh shit, I thought. *I must've left it at security!*

Trying to be rational, I got ahold of the number for Hoedspruit Airport and tried calling, but it turned out they had already closed for the day.

I was in a full-blown panic by this point, and began wandering around the airport like a zombie, trying to get ahold of someone from the TV crew. Eventually, a woman answered, and she actually managed to calm me down by saying, "Don't worry. I'm sure your laptop will be at the airport. One of us will go over there to get it first thing in the morning."

Since I didn't want to buy another expensive plane ticket to L.A. with my own money, I ignored all thoughts of staying overnight in Johannesburg and flying back to Hoedspruit the next morning. Instead, I went over to the business lounge, where I sat

and cried in a corner for five hours, making people stare at me like I was a real weirdo.

The poor staff had to listen to my sad story over and over again. "It's been a really tough day . . . My computer's gone . . ."

When I landed in London after an anxious eight-hour flight, I got a message that almost made me drop to my knees with relief on the asphalt between the airplane and the terminal building: they had found my precious laptop.

33

———

Us Now...

...and our path to the future.

I've tried to help my kids avoid the things I think went wrong with my own childhood, so I make sure they have hobbies, that they're active. My kids take piano, swimming, and tae kwon do classes, and they're not allowed to watch TV during the week. I want to encourage them to do whatever they need to do to feel well and be happy.

In my eyes, it's important and healthy to work. I don't want my kids to work as hard as I do when they're older, but it's important to me that they learn to work hard from a young age. That's the secret behind my success, after all, and the reason I continue to create opportunities for myself.

I'm proud to be here, nearly twenty years later, having paved the way for all the Instagrammers and YouTubers. Before they came along, there was just me. I've outlasted all my peers, all the magazines and TV shows, and I have plenty of great material to discuss with my kids once they're a bit older. They'll probably be hurt, maybe even offended, but that will pass—and quickly. Because the truth is that I love them, they love me, and I've given them a great life.

It's partly for the kids' sake that I still work as hard as I do but also because I enjoy it.

It's partly for the kids' sake that I still work as hard as I do but also because I enjoy it. I enjoy having a routine.

I get up at 5:15 AM five days a week and immediately get to work. The first thing I do is promote my podcast with a video clip, then I check my emails and browse the photo agencies. I have to say that even though it's hard work at times, I'm incredibly grateful that I still get to do this after all these years. I'm particularly grateful for the podcast with Chris Booker and for our listeners. The podcast is different from most others, because we don't have any guests. Our listeners come back to us twice every week to listen to me and Booker, and though he and I have different views on almost everything, he makes me a much better person. I'm so thankful for our collaboration and our friendship, and hope that our podcast can become a TV show at some point.

My kids usually wake up around six thirty, and I sit with them while they eat breakfast. I myself don't eat anything until I've taken the kids to school and been to the gym, which usually takes around an hour and a half.

To avoid losing any more time, I work while I eat. By this point, it's almost eleven o'clock, and I have to catch up on things again. See what I've missed. Give feedback. I have people working

on the website for me now, but I'm still very much involved with
it.

Every video I make takes so long. Writing, editing, upload-
ing . . .

In the afternoon, I have meetings or take part in TV shows.
As much as possible, I try to do at least one unusual thing every
day.

In the evening, I try to give my kids as much quality time as
I can. I always wish I could give them more; I have to make sure
my son does his piano practice, that he reads his books.

I keep working once the kids go to bed. I like to be ahead for the next day, whenever possible, so I also preschedule things for Instagram. I just can't go to bed if I have unanswered emails; I have to answer every last one. If I'm not ahead, I want to be caught up at the very least, because if I'm not caught up, I feel like I'm behind.

When I eventually manage to go to bed, it's usually around one in the morning, meaning I get roughly four and a half hours' sleep a night. That's slightly better than when my website was new, at least; back then, I got around three or four hours' sleep a night.

Sure, it would be nice to work a little less than I do. Eight hours a day instead of sixteen. It would also be great to be able to go on vacation, to really take time off and relax and not—like now—have to work on my days off.

At the same time, being able to work hard is vital to me, because working makes me happy. I'm blessed to do what I do, and sometimes I have to remind myself of that while I'm staring at a screen late at night, and the house is silent after a day of children's voices and buzzing phones—I have to remind myself that I'm awesome, I'm an icon . . . I'm Perez Hilton, bitch!

ACKNOWLEDGMENTS

Perez Hilton thanks:
You . . . seriously. You, reading this right now!

And my friend Erik, who has known me since before I was Perez, and my family and my young niece Mandy.

Martin Svensson & Leif Eriksson thank:
Perez Hilton, Barbara Lavandeira, Teresita Lavandeira, our team, Alice Menzies and Niklas Darke, and our families and friends. All our publishers around the globe, particularly Chicago Review Press, and our agent Daniel Kim at Arena Scripts Literary and Film Agency.